THE END OF
THE WORLD

OFFICIAL WEATHER FORECAST
Fair today and tomorrow; not much change in
temperature; moderate southwest winds.
TEMPERATURE YESTERDAY
Highest 52, 3.45 P. M.; Lowest 30, 8.30 A. M.
(See Complete Report See Editorial Page)

The World

FINAL NEWS EDITION

VOL. LXXI. NO. 25,392—DAILY   Copyright Press Publishing Company (New York World) 1931   NEW YORK, FRIDAY, FEBRUARY 27, 1931   TWO CENTS

Woman Who Offered to Tell About Vice Framing Found Strangled in Park in Bronx

Strangler's Victim—Her Letter

Body of Vivian Gordon, Who Had Tried to Aid Seabury Inquiry, Shows Signs of a Struggle for Life

MAN NAMED IN DIARY TAKEN INTO CUSTODY

"I Fear but One," She Had Written; Taxi Driver Chased Car With Screaming Woman

By Charles F. Stein

Vivian Gordon
VIVIAN GORDON, Who Offered Vice Testimony

FRAZER CONFESSES IN STADER KILLING

Pleads He "Just Happened" to Shoot Sweetheart

DEACONESS AIDED IN A 'VICE' ARREST

But Art Student Held by Mrs. Norris Won Liberty, Married

By Birkman Powell

Mother Speechless 4 Years Exclaims 'My Boy!' as He Shoots Himself Dead

By John W. Butcher

BONUS IS VETOED; HOUSE OVERRIDES HOOVER, 328 - 79

Tilson Howled Down When He Tries to Rally Support for the President

SENATE BALLOTS TODAY; VETO'S DEFEAT EXPECTED

Mills Says Treasury Is Ready to Seek $400,000,000 for First Payments

By Elliott Thornton

BANK INDICTMENTS UPHELD BY COURT; NEW DEFENSE PLAN

Judge Allen Rules Stock Held by Grand Jurors Does Not Impair True Bills

SEPARATE KRESEL TRIAL NEW MOVE OF COUNSEL

Probable Acquittal Would Be Favorable to Other In-dicted Directors

By Allen Raymond

Hurricane Kills 250 In Fiji Isles; Floods Ravage 3 Districts

SUVA, Fiji Islands, Feb. 27

Shaw's Sense of Fun Amazing to Chaplin As They Swap Yarns

By Charlie Chaplin

LONDON, Feb. 26

Scripps-Howard Buy World As Court Permits Sale and Pulitzers Fulfill Contract

Statement by the Trustees On Sale of World Papers

Surrogate Foley Renders De-cision on Plea to Break Will, but Refuses to Pass Public Support

THE TRUSTEES SET ASIDE Papers—Staff's Fund Wins Public Support

Stern and Gannett Bid for

The World, The Evening World and The Sunday World have been sold to the Scripps-Howard interests, owners of the New York Telegram.

By Lindesay Parrott

RALPH PULITZER
JOSEPH PULITZER
HERBERT PULITZER
Trustees

CAUCUS RENAMES OFFICERS OF HOUSE

Longworth and Tilson Ac-claimed at G. O. P. Meeting

By The World's Bureau
WASHINGTON, Feb. 26

BUYER OF WORLD STATES POLICIES

Howard Promises Loyalty to Scripps and Pulitzer Ideals

Buy W. Return of the Scripps-Howard chain of newspapers.

Ship Lines Cut Rates to Europe So Jobless Aliens Can Go Home

Gen. Pershing Tells How Troop Shift Displeased British

A LAST FRONT PAGE

THE END OF

The World

A POST-MORTEM

By

Its Intangible Assets

JAMES W. BARRETT

OF THE CITY DESK

EDITOR

HARPER & BROTHERS PUBLISHERS
NEW YORK AND LONDON   1931

THE END OF *THE WORLD*
Copyright, 1931, by Harper & Brothers
Printed in the U. S. A.
SECOND PRINTING
D-F

DEDICATED TO
NEWSPAPERMEN EVERYWHERE
WHO LOVED
The World

The ⬤ World   DAY ASSIGNMENT SCHEDULE   (CITY DEPARTMENT)

City Editor __James W. Barrett__   ____Friday, February 27th____ 1931

Day City Editor __Alex Schlosser__   Night City Editor __Ben Franklin__

Copy Readers __Harper & Brothers__

Binders Margin	NAME OF REPORTER	SUBJECT	Sent Out	Turned In	Space	Page
	Barrett	Foreword				1
	F. P. A.	The World Was Too Much With Us.				16
	Paulin	The World We Lived In				27
	Montague	The Last Supper				41
	Schechter	The World for Sale				59
	Gibbs	Enter Don Quixotes				70
	Michelson	The Hell Box Edition of The Sunday World				91
	Schlosser	The Last Day				99
	Garrison & Genauer	The Death Watch at Surrogate's Court				110
	Franklin	The Last Night				116
	Parrott	The Last Story				127
	Leary	City Room				136
	Davidson	At Daly's				150
	Nichols	Sic Transit Gloria Mundi				162
	Lippman	Valedictory				178
	Littell	Curtain				181
	Chotzinoff	A First Assignment				187
	Sullivan	Thoughts Before the Undertaker Came				195
	Pearl	The World Passes				206
	Broun	It Seemed to Me				214
	Parker	Just Break the News				220
	McCormick	Doomsday				231
	Kober	Portrait of the Artist as a Corpse				241
	Rogers	Some Legal Aspects				251
	Hansen	The Last Reader				257
	Barrett	On Abraham's Bosom				267
	Kan	Obituary				270

Do not write in this space or cut off any part of this schedule

NIGHT ASSIGNMENTS

OVERNIGHT ASSIGNMENTS

Illustrations

THE END OF
THE WORLD

FOREWORD

By The City Editor

PROBABLY my chief weakness as a New York newspaper man is a regrettable tendency to become involved in news situations instead of preserving toward them that complete impartiality and objectivity which is so highly commended by our best schools of journalism.

In the Rockland County investigation I became entangled as a witness for the prosecution; in the Oliver Osborne case I got mixed up with the defense; and as city editor of the *World* I slipped from even-mindedness more times than I like to think about.

Every one of these lapses—all violations of Canon No. 65-23-44-A of the Principles of Journalism—were followed by poignant remorse, but still the fault remained; and on the occasion of my greatest ordeal—the covering of the death of my own paper—it broke out again in a most disgraceful manner. Instead

1

of remaining dutifully at the city desk of the *World* on February 24, 25, and 26 last, to direct the assignments in connection with the sale of the Pulitzer newspapers, I went out and took a part in the drama.

This was as great a newspaper blunder as it would be for Bob Littell to get up out of his seat in a theater to take one of the parts in a play instead of remaining in the audience as dramatic critic; or for Chotzinoff to horn into the Philharmonic Symphony Orchestra or into the chorus of the Metropolitan Opera instead of staying in the Bill Guard sector; or for Elliott Thurston to descend to the floor of the United States Senate for the purpose of filling the *Congressional Record* instead of remaining in the press gallery.

For this unforgivable lapse I have repented in gunny sacks and ashes, but the shame of it will never be erased; and my guilty conscience is not helped at all by the knowledge that practically everybody else in the *World* organization stayed at his post through those three hectic days and nights with no other thought than to get the regular news of those days into the paper. Members of the editorial

2

staff as a whole were so busy doing their regular jobs that they had little time to worry about what was happening to the *World*; only the city editor got excited.

It should be understood that when the *World* was sold, it was not regarded in the news-rooms of the *World* as a specially big story. Everybody had known for a long time that the paper was on the skids and that its importance was becoming less and less every day—so that when it was finally sold, the general idea was that it was a fairly good first-page story, but probably not so important as the Bank of United States or the Seabury investigation stories. Not until the first editions of the *Times* and the *Herald Tribune* came into the *World* office on the morning of February 25 did we begin to realize that the end of the *World* might possibly be a great big story. I might add that this failure to grab hold of a "hot" story before seeing the first editions of the other papers was not untypical of the *World* in its latter days—which may explain why some of us thought that it did not make much difference whether the paper was sold or not. On the eve of the sale, the *World* was

not much more than a shell of its former self.
Just before its extinction it came back to life
as its old self and for three days lived and
functioned superbly, and finally went out in
a sunset blaze of glory—which makes it all
the more deplorable that the city editor should
have fallen down.

By way of making partial amends for the
most important slip-up in my newspaper life
—barring those that are to come—I have
asked the staff of the *World*—past and present—to do the story of the end of the *World*
all over again, and this time I promise not to
run out on the job. Sitting as city editor for
the occasion, I have, I think, covered every
angle of the story by assigning a brilliant man
or woman to write it up. What we failed to do
in the last issues of the paper we may achieve
here—if not it will certainly not be for lack
of genius.

Looking back at it, one can see that the
staff of the *World* really never had a chance
to cover its death adequately. In the first place,
there was no prepared obituary material in
type ready to throw into the paper on an instant's notice, as there was in the offices of

the *Times* and the *Herald Tribune*. Those papers prepared for the death of the *World* just as they do for the death of a famous man. That is to say, they had complete background in the way of biography, history, and illustrations. The *World*, as I recall it, gave about half a column of its own biography, and while the *Times* and *Herald Tribune* carried photographs of Ralph, Joseph, and Herbert Pulitzer, and pictures of the World Building appeared in several papers, the *World* itself made no use of any of them. We did not even use the mats and reading-matter sent out by the Associated Press.

Then, too, nobody could write in the columns of the *World* or any other daily newspaper the emotions of the editors and staff as they went about the task of preparing the last editions of their own paper. Possibly, at that actual time we had no emotions at all, except a dim sense that something terrible was happening somewhere, and that we had no time to figure out just what it was. In fact, most of us could not believe that it was indeed the end of the *World*, and even if we were inclined to

5

believe it, we lacked the time—there was so much else to be done.

On the last day of the *World's* existence there was so much else to be covered, so many other big stories, that we had to slight the *World* story. On the last day of the *World* the Vivian Gordon story broke. That was the story of the woman of the underworld whose body was found at the foot of an embankment in Van Cortlandt Park. She had been strangled. "Her murder," the *World* said in its last issue, "threw the police authorities in the greatest tumult the city has seen since the killing of Herman Rosenthal in 1912." Vivian Gordon had volunteered to tell her story of a police frame-up to the Seabury inquiry, but she did not even get near the witness stand. The underworld saw to that.

Well, that certainly was a story, and you can't blame the acting day city editor, Alex Schlosser, for thinking it was more important than the sale of the *World*. He assigned Charley Stutz, one of our best though not highest-salaried men, to cover the murder and at the same time notified Hickman Powell, author of *The Last Paradise* (no reference to the

World) to cover all developments bearing on the Seabury investigation, to which Powell was regularly assigned. I should note in passing that things were so regular in the *World* office on the last day of its existence that Tom Hanly, the regular day city or assignment editor, was taking his regular day off; John T. Gibbs, who covered the *World* story the day before, was taking his regular day off, and Phil Pearl, who covered the story on the first day, was taking a day off due in accordance with regulations.

Sayre B. Rose, younger staff member, who might have been available for certain angles of the *World* sale story, was assigned to assist Stutz.

We might have assigned Allen Norton, a thoroughly competent though explosive man, to do the honors on the end-of-the-*World* job, but Mr. Norton was tied up with the Bank of United States and it was impossible to engage his attention with other matters. And it so happened on this particular day that Judge Allen in General Sessions upheld indictments against eight former officials of the defunct bank.

7

In the Kresel or Seabury inquiry, as we variously called it, there was plenty doing. A twenty-year-old art student and model went on the witness stand and testified as to how her Greenwich Village romance was broken up through the agency of a Methodist Church deaconess and a policewoman, working in this case in a partnership combining the worst features of each.

Two hundred Communists started a parade for Albany to ask Governor Roosevelt to do something about unemployment. Lena Burlott, the wandering Bedford alumna, returned home after an alleged kidnapping. Lena bestowed plenty of trouble on the *World* in its latter days. A Queens grocer was killed in a hold-up. . . . Presiding Justice Lazansky wrote a letter to Governor Roosevelt, telling him that the magistrates in Brooklyn are all right . . . so is Ben Marvin, though the P. J. didn't mention him. . . . Passage of the veterans' bonus bill over Hoover's veto called for a round-up of local opinion and local preparations for administering the loans. . . . Transatlantic steamship lines cut their third-class rates as a first aid to jobless immigrants . . .

this may help some *World* men later on. . . .
More physicians facing indictment for liquor
violations. . . . Eighteen men indicted in Nas-
sau County for rum-running. . . . How in
God's name can we cover all the news and still
give proper attention to the selling of our own
paper?

Assignments are supposed to be the proof
of a city editor's genius. Some people, including John J. Leary, Jr., writing in the *Editor
& Publisher*, attribute great forethought and
discrimination to yours truly because Lindesay
Parrott was picked to cover and write the last
day of the *World*. Mr. Parrott was not, strictly
speaking, a *World* man. He had come to us
only a few weeks previously, from the *Evening
Post*, and returned to that paper immediately
after the *World* collapse. Mr. Leary thought
I deliberately picked an "outsider" to cover
the end of the *World* because his feelings
would not be involved. I can assure Mr. Leary
and everyone else that I was guilty of no such
shrewdness. In the first place, the selection of
Mr. Parrott was purely an accident; he happened to be the only available man after the
other news assignments of the day had been

made. In the second place, Alex Schlosser picked him, not I, because at that particular time I was off the job, glued to a telephone in a lawyer's office, trying to raise subscriptions to enable the *World* employees to make an offer to buy the paper from the Pulitzer brothers.

This is not to disparage the job done by Mr. Parrott. It was first class. His narrative is included in the present round-up.

And now, since every delinquent is entitled to his day in court—vice squad notwithstanding—may I say just a word as to why I went loco during the greatest crisis in the life of my newspaper?

For weeks before the end of the paper the *World* office had been shaken by successive rumors of an impending sale as though by the tremors that precede an earthquake. There were two distinct shocks. Mr. John G. Jackson, counsel for the Pulitzer trustees, said in the Surrogate's Court that the morale of the *World* staff was broken. I shall not attempt to characterize Mr. Jackson. His statement speaks for itself. His statement is the best evidence of what he knew about the spirit of the *World*.

I wonder what he thought when he read the last three issues of the *World* and found them perfect from the standpoint of newspaper workmanship.

The fact is that, up to the time of the sale, the morale of the *World* staff was shaken but unbroken. How could it remain unshaken when we knew that there was "something doing" and yet we received positive assurances that all such rumors were false?

If any condemnation is to be handed out in connection with the sale of the *World*—and goodness knows I am not condemning anybody—it should be bestowed upon the decision not to take into confidence the men and women who had given years of faithful and efficient service. The reason for secrecy probably was stated by Roy Howard on the witness stand before Surrogate Foley when he testified:

"The publicity that has attended this hearing will inevitably be communicated to the staff of the *World*. It is obvious that it will bring a very serious confusion and disintegration in that organization."

Mr. Howard has admitted privately since

11

then that this was a serious mistake on his part. How seriously he and others misjudged the *World* staff was shown by the whole-hearted spirit in which they entered the task of getting out the last issues of their paper. Was there perhaps a fear on somebody's part that the *World* employees would commit sabotage? The ugly word was whispered.

How little any of the "higher-ups" knew about *World* reporters! How little did they imagine that we could take it on the chin with a smile, so far as our own jobs were concerned, and reserve our tears for the great newspaper institution ". . . an institution that should always fight for progress and reform" . . . "always remain devoted to the public welfare" . . . "never be satisfied with merely printing news" . . . "never be afraid to attack wrong" . . . reserve our tears and our everlasting love for the thing which Joseph Pulitzer created through genius and suffering and which these gentlemen permitted to be destroyed.

When the proceedings before Surrogate Foley publicly disclosed that the *World* was indeed for sale—had actually been sold, sub-

ject to the Surrogate's approval—then indeed
we realized how greatly we had been fooled
by all those assurances that no such sale was
in prospect. Opinion in the office was divided.
Some said we should "sit tight" and go
through to the end without a protest. Others
urged a public protest. My own inclination at
first was follow the admirable example of Mr.
Ralph E. Renaud, managing editor, who for
two years did his job and kept a stiff upper
lip like the Spartan youth, though a fox was
gnawing at his vitals. But the spirit of protest
became insistent. The boys and girls whose
work had made it possible for me to be a city
editor seemed to be looking to me . . . they
seemed to be saying, though they didn't put it
in words:

"We stood by you. . . . Are you going to
stand by us? Are you going to let us be thrown
out into the breadline and the scrap-heap without uttering a protest? Do the friendships, the
pleasant associations, the little luncheon gath-
erings at Racky's mean nothing to you? Are
you the Little Father of our bunch? Will you
remain silent when everything that newspaper

men and newspaper women respect calls for action?"

No, no! A thousand times no!

Gustavus Rogers on the telephone offers to intervene for us if we will sign an authorization. Can't do it for an anonymous client . . . must have names . . . will we sign? The paper goes through the office like a city-news bulletin. Everybody signs it, from Earl Clauson, day managing editor, down to the office boys . . . that is, almost everybody. Why bother about the exceptions? Mr. Rogers must know by one o'clock and here it is twelve-fifty. . . . I get him on the telephone. . . . Go ahead full steam. . . . Damn the duties and the responsibilities! Rogers wants to know what are the facts, what is the case, where can he get a copy of the will. . . . All too late . . . no time for legal preparation. . . . Meet him in the Surrogate's Court right away . . . ten minutes for conference. . . . Did ever barrister so rash a deed?

Foley is sympathetic, but his job is to decide a legal question. He permits Rogers to sit in with the other lawyers. We get a respite . . . too short. We get $600,000 in pledges before dawn, but it is all useless. The trustees are bound by contract to sell and Scripps-Howard is bound by contract to buy.

The only chance the so-called employees had was in the remote possibility that both parties might hold back or withdraw by mutual consent and let the employees try to raise the money to take over the paper. But that apparently was not even considered.

I shall disclose a little secret here, now that it is all over. Had we been given our chance we would have produced not one million dollars, but ten millions. Some day I may tell you the name of the man who agreed to put up the ten millions.

That was how the city editor went loco just before his finish, and so far as I am concerned —if that was treason, make the most of it! But everybody else did his job splendidly and stayed with the paper . . . "even unto the end of the *World*."

And now let us get on with the story. Here is the assignment schedule:

Here is a shrewd post mortem, written by one of the World's *distinguished contributors who describes the attractions and the fatal weaknesses of the paper as he watched them for nine years.*

THE *WORLD* WAS TOO MUCH WITH US

By *Franklin P. Adams*

"Who killed the *World*?"
 "I," said J. P.,
  "With my last will and t.,—
I killed the *World*."

WHO saw it die?"
  "I," said 2,867 of us.

I cannot fill in the hiatus between the will of Joseph Pulitzer and the final edition of February 27, 1931. And neither can Bennett, Galsworthy, Dreiser, Sinclair Lewis, Sigmund Freud, Silas Bent, the Audit Bureau of Circulation—not any of them, or all of them put together. It is too tragic, too comic a story; it is too complex. Since February 27, 1931, I have seen dozens of written theories and in-

16

quest reports; none was absurd, and none was all true. Yet most of them were written by men who had worked for a newspaper that was supposed to be passionately truthful and accurate. For the truth about the *World* is that there is so much truth to be told that no man could tell it all; for some of it soars into the rarefied ether of metaphysics, or the half-drunk realm of wild speculation. Anybody half-competent to write about the *World* or to diagnose the disease that resulted in its utter and complete death is likely to be partisan; he is likely to be too bitter or too sentimental. He wants, perhaps unconsciously, to bite the hands that fed him; or to pat the hand that struck him and snatched the bread from his mouth.

My candidate to write the story is Ralph Pulitzer. If he wrote it as I would like to see it written—and it would be fascinating reading—he would have to risk the friendship of most of his friends and the love, amity, or lack of open enmity—whatever the fraternal status might be at the time—of his entire family. He would have to risk the even greater thing: what would his father—and his mother—

think? And he would have to be courageous, candid, excessively industrious and patient; traits which he possesses, though I doubt in such conspicuous degree as to enable him to do such a heart-breaking job. But nobody else can approach Ralph Pulitzer in the latent ability to write such a book.

If I were asked—and it seems to me that I have been asked, though this is the first assignment that the city editor of the *World* ever gave me—to say what the *World* died of, I should say that Joseph Pulitzer created it and killed it; that J. P. gave, and J. P. took away. There is no doubt that Joseph Pulitzer was a great journalist, nor that he had courage. But I think that he was a man who must have been torn by misgivings as to his own power and ability; that these doubts and fears so dominated him that he was incapable of trusting anybody; and by trust I mean the last limit of trust.

For years I took Joseph Pulitzer on faith. When I came to the *World* on January 1, 1922, I noticed the great height of the window base from the floor. I was told that the windows in the editorial rooms had been con-

structed by Joseph Pulitzer's wish, so that reporters and editorial-writers should not be
tempted to gaze out of the window, thus
neglecting their work. That, I thought, was a
mere idiosyncrasy of genius. It was, I believe,
the actuating force of his journalistic career
as it affected the paper and those who were
supposed to run it after his death. Certainly it
never seemed to me that, by the terms of his
will, he had trusted the sons—any of them—
enough to let them run his papers independ-
ently of him. Militant for the independence of
journalism, he yet forced his sons to be de-
pendent upon him; to depend upon his independence, so that they must automatically
have been robbed of any great independence
of their own.

That, however, was what the will and testament did. Probably the Greek tragedians
would have seen clearly the night of February 26, 1931, when the Pulitzer boys were
born. I have no idea what the boyhood and
childhood of Ralph, Joseph, and Herbert
Pulitzer were; but I doubt that there was that
emotional stability that makes a happy childhood. I should think that there must have

been great ups and downs; alternate spoil-
ings and humiliating punishments. . . . Let
me add that all these are speculations and
guesses. Nobody ever told me a word about the
bringing up of those boys. I think it was pater-
nal distrust of the boys that doomed the
paper, for the boys naturally found it difficult not to distrust everybody, no matter how
slightly.

Into those things I am not, as may have
been discovered, wise enough or diplomatic
enough to go deeper. I know this: that considering the handicaps under which I assume that
Ralph Pulitzer came to the editorship of the
World, the courage, industry, and patience
he exhibited seemed to me enormous. Under
the same conditions, I think most of us
wouldn't have worked at all, or would have
given up in a year, instead of twenty. It
seemed to me many times that it took too long
for him to decide, and that there were too few
of us in the office who knew him. The reporters, the men who made his paper, didn't
know him; most of them never had—never
have seen him. As to autopsies, this one is
longer than I had intended; but there was

hardly a day while I was there—nine years
and two months—that I didn't feel that the
paper could easily have been better with slight
effort. And it was my saying so that taught
me that you couldn't get past what I used to
call, after my first three months, the ghost of
Joseph Pulitzer. The Pulitzer Building was a
haunted house.

And now a major chord. Never had I known
such fun in a newspaper office as I had the first
few years on the *World*. Whatever office politics there may have been, I was unaffected, for
nobody wanted my job and I didn't want anybody's. When I came there Heywood Broun
and I, who had been co-slaves on the *Tribune*,
divided three columns on the page opposite
the editorial. That page was Herbert Swopes'
idea, and it was to be, he says that he said, a
page of opinion. Broun did a column called "It
Seems to Me," and the dramatic reviews.
Broun's column was a journalistic phenome-
non; he is, I think, one of the great journalists
of all time. And the greatest tribute he ever got
he never knew; this is his first intimation.

As late as 1930, three years after he had
been discharged for alleged disloyalty, after

dozens of pinch-hitters, substitutes, and more
or less permanencies did their three-a-week
best—Elsie McCormick, William Bolitho,
Robert Littell—everybody, from the dis-
charger down, generally referred to it as "the
Broun column." I took a shot at getting people
to write for it during the summer of 1930, and
people on the staff always gave it to me for
"the Broun column." I want it on the record
that firing Broun, for anything, was a mistake.

Then Deems Taylor came on to write about
music. I had a cubicle. Taylor and Broun and
Alison Smith, assistant music critic and assistant dramatic critic, had another. I came to
the office every day, and they came most days.
Often there were discussions and violent, abu-
sive arguments lasting three hours. Broun
stopped writing dramatic stuff, and Alexander
Woollcott wrote fine stuff—the stuff that only
a stage-struck or a theater-bored critic can
write.

In the rarer atmosphere of the Dome there
was Frank Cobb during my first year or two.
Cobb came to my desk the first day and said,
"Christ! a newspaper man! I thought you
were one of those damn prima donnas that

worked at home and sent it in by messenger."
He would stop almost every morning to comment on some verse or paragraph. Sometimes
it would be, "You ought to know better than
to write a futile paragraph like that; it's false
philosophy." And once in a while, "I'd give
my shirt if I could put that punch in two lines.
Damn! that's art. Glad you're on the same
paper." But the stimulation of his violent interest was terrific.

There were the arguments I used to have
with reporters, hour after hour in the city
room, about critics; with Oliver Garrett, Dudley Nichols, and Charley Hand. It was always
my first day in the office, and nothing about it
bored me. I used to argue with my boss on this
job, Jimmy Barrett, as to why we didn't have
this story or why we emphasized that. We
didn't have the story, usually, because we
didn't have the reporters, and we didn't have
the reporters because we didn't have the
money. There were fights—generally telephone—with my technical boss, Mr. Swope,
sir, who never changed a line, in or out, of
mine, except once, when he saved me, by
changing something that had become untrue

between the time that I wrote it, at 3 P.M.,
and 8:30 P.M. There was fun with Frank Sullivan, and fun bedeviling Louis Weitzenkorn.
There was great and affectionate respect for
John L. Heaton, and a lasting friendship for
Walter Lippmann, who, I imagine, fought
harder for more justice for more people on the
World than anybody else; and for more of
them than most of them knew, or ever will
know.

There was Rollin Kirby, with whom I had
an agreement to finish work by 2:30 so that
we might hurry uptown for a game of pool.
People who used to compliment Kirby on the
simplicity of his cartoons didn't know that one
figure meant two o'clock, two figures 2:30,
and a lot of figures no pool at all. There was
Alex Schloesser, who knew more about the
office personnel, not to say all stories in all the
papers, than anybody else. He was Gibraltar;
he never failed anybody. There were Ayres
and Cooper and the other boys in the room
with the stock-tickers, who even on the last
day yelled, "Well, kid, General Electric is
down one-eighth, but the *World* hits a new
low for all time. Well, no work tomorrow!"

24

There were those unforgettable last three days when we were told, about three o'clock Tuesday afternoon, that the hearing would take place at 4:15, and that by 4:45 we ought to Know All. Postponement. Next morning the Block "offer." Postponement. Thursday noon the employees' "offer," with Jimmy Barrett in the Surrogate's Court, seeing his boss, Herbert Pulitzer, for, I think, the first time. And then that aching night when I waited in Lippmann's office, in Renaud's office, at home, at the pool table with Kirby, at the office, at Swope's house. From there I called up the office and learned of the sale to Roy Howard. Howard had said that he didn't want me, and for the first time in my newspaper-column career— twenty-seven and one-half years—I had no job, and no money, and a wife, two hungry children, and two houses. But there was no *World.* It was not to be borne. They had been telling us, for two years, that it was coming. I didn't believe it. I didn't believe it that night.

Next day many persons—contributors and others—telephoned to find out why the *World* didn't still come out on Saturday morning. "Why," said a lady from Newark, "where's the *World?*" My wife said it had been sold. "I read that," she said, "but somebody *bought* it!" My wife said it had been bought by Scripps-Howard and would be known as the *World-Telegram.* "But how," asked this stranger, "do I know what your husband has been doing all week?" She was told that the *World* actually had ceased, and that I had no job. "Why," she said, "they can't do that! I'll take it to the Supreme Court!" And that morning seventy-one others telephoned my house to know why the *World* had gone off the newsstands. Thousands of persons that we in the office never dreamed felt that way said it was as though somebody in the family had died— yes, had been murdered.

On my last day in the *World* office I wrote a rhyme about Journalism. It was the way I felt about the *World.* Thus:

Journalism's a shrew and scold;
    I like her.
She makes you sick, she makes you old;
    I like her.
She's daily trouble, stress and strife;
She's Love and Hate and Death and Life;
She ain't no lady—she's my wife—
    I like her.

26

One of the essentials in covering a news story is background. Mr. Paulin, editorial writer under Joseph Pulitzer, Frank I. Cobb, and Walter Lippmann, gives here a picture of the World *that made tradition.*

THE *WORLD* WE LIVED IN

By L. R. E. Paulin

WHEN Joseph Pulitzer bought the *World* from Jay Gould in May, 1883, it was a decrepit and moribund sheet. He converted it into a newspaper that was to be a powerful influence in shaping public opinion in the United States. While he was a great editor in every sense, in the handling of news and weighing of passing events, it was to the editorial page that he gave his chief attention. Always he was fired by the principles which he proclaimed at the top of the editorial page:

As an institution that should always fight for progress and reform, never tolerate injustice or corruption, always fight demagogues of all parties, never belong to any party, always oppose privileged classes and public plunderers, never lack

27

sympathy with the poor, always remain devoted to the public welfare, never be satisfied with merely printing news, always be drastically independent, never be afraid to attack wrong, whether by predatory plutocracy or predatory poverty.

While he adhered to this general program, he never made a fetish of mere consistency. He was not afraid to express warm admiration of public men, and then on occasion to criticize them sharply. No one at times praised Theodore Roosevelt more highly; none more completely exposed his weaknesses and ridiculed his pretensions to statesmanship. Both Taft and Hughes were objects of his high approval at certain periods of their careers; at others they came under the lash of his criticism. More than anything else, Mr. Pulitzer insisted that the *World* be independent in its judgment, free from partisan bias and party allegiance. At heart he was a Democrat by conviction. No one more savagely lashed the Democratic party when it was guilty of cowardice or unfaithfulness to principle.

Mr. Pulitzer had that rare gift of leadership which inspired those with whom he worked with his own zeal and energy. In any

emergency he was at the front of his band of
editors, more active, more fertile in ideas,
more persistent and pugnacious than any of
them could be. It was never any question of
getting the best out of them that they had to
give, for they knew that "the old man" was
contributing out of his own brain more than
his editors could pretend to offer. After blindness overtook him, he was constantly on the
move, traveling on his yacht, but always by
cable or otherwise he kept in touch with the
World. By wire, by written messages, he
poured suggestions and criticisms upon the
men "in the Dome" who were actually writing
the editorials in the *World*. He was generous
in his praise of their work, merciless in condemning what he considered their blunders,
and verbally unrestrained whenever he de-
tected signs of careless or evasive writing. But
with all his impatience he was generous at
heart and kindly in thought, and his personal
interest in the members of the *World* staff was
constantly a surprise to them when in casual
conversation he referred to minor incidents or
private matters which a busy man ordinarily
would forget, if told.

To those in close association with him he was a daily puzzle. Sometimes he was in violent eruption, sometimes he was quiet and docile as a well-behaved child, but he could change from one manner to the other without warning. On first acquaintance some of his peculiarities of manner were disturbing. He was always likely to do the unexpected. On impulse, he called for information which required long research, overlooked previous requests or suggestions that he had made, and apparently followed the whim of the moment. But those who knew him best over a long period of years found in him always the same amazing curiosity and eagerness for information, retentive memory for essential facts, and startling rapidity in speech and action.

There can be little doubt that, after his blindness, when he was served by a corps of highly trained secretaries, he developed a sense of which few persons are possessed. In the darkness he could see further, with the aid of imagination, than others; he was more conscious of personal mannerisms in speech and conduct; he was also quicker to irritation, more impatient of stupidity; and he was not

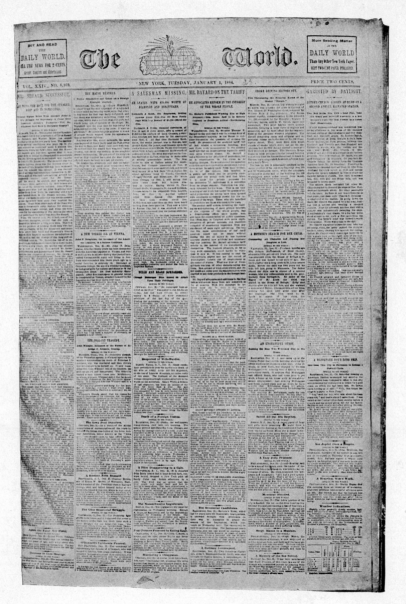

AS IT WAS UNDER J. P.

without a certain malicious delight in trapping
in argument those from whom he sought advice
or assistance.

All of these idiosyncrasies were the cause
of no little amusement among the members of
his editorial staff, and at times of great distress of mind and resentment. He would admit that he did not expect all his directions to
be acted upon in a spirit of implicit obedience.
He held the men on the ground responsible for
exercising their own judgment according to
the circumstances at the moment. He would
have held in contempt an editor who did not
have the courage and self-assertion to go beyond instructions and decide important questions on the spur of the occasion. It was characteristic of him that, while he might criticize
past performances, his mind was fixed on the
future, and his words of guidance were directed
to shaping policy ahead of events.

William H. Merrill, the veteran editor, at
one time head of the *Boston Herald,* was long
in charge of the editorial page. Among the
members of his staff were John A. Dillon,
George Cary Eggleston, David Graham Phil-
lips, Sam Moffett (Mark Twain's nephew),

and John L. Heaton. Mr. Merrill was a placid and handsome old gentleman, an accomplished writer of large experience, with a profound knowledge of Amerian politics and history, but Mr. Pulitzer had the faculty of throwing him off his balance. Sometimes when an avalanche of notes would arrive from the Pulitzer headquarters, wherever it might be, "Pop" Merrill would retire into himself until his nerves were quieted and, with a smiling face, he felt capable of alloting the tasks assigned to the various editors of the staff. He was not the bold, daring, and impetuous person that Frank Cobb, his successor, was.

Cobb, who was brought on from the *Detroit Free Press* in 1904, was a big, strong, active man, given to tremendous bursts of energy and quick decisions. He had a way of dashing around the corridor of the fifteenth floor of the Dome, opening the door of an editorial-writer's room, throwing off a hasty remark, and disappearing. All the while in his head he was shaping a leading editorial on some topic of the day. He might discuss it by bits with anyone whom he met, pour out sentences conceived on the run, and keep this up perhaps at the lunch table or on chance meetings. Late in the afternoon he would retire to his room, lock the door, sit down at his typewriter, and bang out an editorial a column long in half an hour.

Cobb and Mr. Pulitzer were in the habit of engaging in furious argument. They had much the same vociferousness of manner, headlong speech, and trick of over-assertion; but out of this clash of minds there grew a spirit of perfect understanding and coöperation and a feeling of strong respect and affection on both sides. Cobb was perhaps the most able and versatile editorial writer that American journalism has produced since the opening of the present century. He was dogmatic in tone, but always open to reason and information, the only man of the kind I have ever known. With that, he had tremendous dash, invention, and resourcefulness, a keen eye for news, shrewd political sense, and power of clear and forceful expression. He was a magnetic, inspiring person, to whom his associates looked with confidence for helpful and heartening leadership. His death was an irreparable loss to the *World* and to American journalism. Among

33

his associates, after he took charge of the
editorial page, were John L. Heaton, L. R. E.
Paulin, A. B. Kingsbury, Horatio Seymour,
Ernest H. Howard, and E. W. Osborn. It was
the practice for each editorial-writer to cover
a particular field, although they frequently
overlapped. Seymour was a veteran who had
long served with Joseph Story in Chicago and
had been editor of the *Chicago Journal.* He
had an inexhaustible knowledge of American
politics. Heaton knew more about municipal
and state government in New York and social
and industrial history than all the others.
Kingsbury had a delightfully light touch for
social and literary topics, and Osborn had long
dealt with the theater and local affairs. Paulin
wrote chiefly on foreign affairs and Washington politics and legislation. It was a well-
rounded staff of men who were held closely together by friendship as well as by faith in the
World's ideals and methods.

It was always an interesting experience
when a budget of notes arrived from Mr.
Pulitzer. He might be on his yacht on the
Riviera, he might be at Bar Harbor or Jekyl
Island. The notes transcribed by his secretary

came by hand, by mail, or by wire. One famous collection arrived when the yacht *Liberty* had crossed the Atlantic and was reported at Bar Harbor. There were some sixty pages of it, written down day by day on the voyage home, as a large bundle of copies of the *World* had been thrashed over by Mr. Pulitzer and his secretary. These notes, as they related to one editorial-writer or another, were sorted out and delivered to them, and they were the cause of much entertainment to the staff.

I remember one message to Cobb: "During Heaton's absence, Cobb has entire charge of the editorial page, but I beg, insist, that he will personally not write one word about Socialism, Bryanism, Dingleyism, the tariff protection, the question of railroad rates, political economy, or any abstract academic subject, interesting only to few. I especially beg him to cultivate a vein of irony, diminish very long editorials which have become chronic, also avoid superlatives like: 'monstrous,' 'traitor,' 'anarchist,' etc., as rather juvenile, feeble." 1592755

I recall one message directed to me some time after I had written an editorial on the railroad question during the Roosevelt administration before the matter had become a live issue. It ran to this effect: "Tell Paulin when he goes to his home on Staten Island and returns to look in the faces of the different people and ask himself how many of them either read these articles or would not be more interested in many other topics." Within a year President Roosevelt had realized the full importance of the railroad issue and Mr. Pulitzer was soon in the van in calling for effective legislation. He did not bother to remember what he had said a few months before, and if he did, it didn't matter. A subject that was negligible in January might be of first importance to him in June.

One experience that I had with Mr. Pulitzer revealed to me the groping of the blind man's mind for knowledge beyond his reach. He wanted an answer where no answer was to be had, and he could not get away from the subject. It was at the time of the war between Russia and Japan. Admiral Rojestvensky had sailed with the Russian fleet for the Far East. He had stopped at Madagascar to refuel and remained there several weeks. One day without warning the Russian fleet put to sea. All over the world, military critics and newspapers, were puzzled to say what his next destination might be, whether he was turning back for the Baltic or headed for Japan to meet Togo. A brief note came from Mr. Pulitzer, saying "Tell Paulin every day to have editorial locating Rojestvensky's fleet." It was an impossible task, and at best one could only throw out cautious surmises as to where the Russians were going and what their intentions were. For three weeks it was my daily duty to write a few words without any real knowledge of the Russians' purpose. They might be headed westward, they might be crossing the Indian Ocean; no one could say. But Mr. Pulitzer was feeling about blindly for some fact on which to form an opinion as to the conclusion of the war. He knew what none of us clearly realized, that here was a great mystery, a strong fleet at sea which might confess failure in advance and return to Europe, or which might venture all on one throw and challenge Japan's navy in its home waters.

Unexpectedly, one day, "a news flash" announced that Rojestvensky's fleet had been

sighted in the Straits of Singapore. At once
came a message from Mr. Pulitzer: "Have
Paulin for me say that Togo will wipe the Russians off the sea when and where he chooses
to meet them." No editor in his senses would
have dared to make such a rash prediction. Mr.
Pulitzer uttered it without the slightest quali-
fication. He took what seemed to the rest of
us to be an inexcusable risk and delivered himself of a preconceived opinion without the
slightest warrant. The rest of us had been dis-
creetly following the lead of British and American naval authorities in comparing the ton-
nage and strength in guns of the Russian and
Japanese fleets without presuming to say what
would be the outcome of a great naval battle,
if they should meet. It was only ordinary prudence to await events. Mr. Pulitzer threw
prudence to the winds. He was right. When
Togo fell upon Rojestvensky at the chosen
spot he wiped the Russians off the sea.

After the death of Mr. Pulitzer in 1911, it
fell to Frank Cobb to direct the editorial policy
of the *World* almost up to the time of his death
in 1925. He maintained its vigorous, outspoken, and fearless tone to the last. Before

Cobb's death, owing to changes in the editorial staff, it became evident that some younger man must be called in. Walter Lippmann was put in charge of the editorial page. As assistants Charles Merz and John L. Heaton served. Other members of the staff were Allan Nevins, W. O. Scroggs, James M. Cain, and L. R. E. Paulin. Rollin Kirby, who had been the distinguished cartoonist of the *World* for many years, continued until the last issue. The *World*, as ever, was a persistent advocate of international conciliation, limited armaments, and the readjustment of war reparation claims. It fought corruption in the national administration and in the New York City government with its accustomed vigor and uncompromising persistence. If its tone was somewhat more polite and less venomous than in the days of Mr. Pulitzer's prime, it was none the less the same leader in shaping public opinion, in national politics, and in public affairs. It riddled the claims made for prohibition as a great moral reform; it upheld the principle of self-government for the states; it attacked corruption in official and political life as a result of the false reformers' efforts

to abolish the liquor traffic by constitutional
and legal decree; it died fighting, and it left
many a bruised and bloody head behind it at
the time that it ceased publication.

The one doctrine which the *World* preached,
in and out of season from the time Mr. Pulitzer
took it over from Jay Gould to the day of its
suspension, was the furtherance of peace by
international effort. This purpose was clearly
indicated in Mr. Pulitzer's own initial utter-
ances in 1883. It was no less emphatically
upheld in the last days of the *World*. The fight
against privilege, against unjust taxation,
wasteful expenditure, corruption in public
office, was steadfastly maintained by the
World throughout its long life. It was an
ardent fighter in behalf of many candidates
for office and many party causes, but it never
sacrificed its own freedom of judgment or independence of action to party expediency. It
may have been at times mistaken, even preju-
diced, in some of its judgments, but it was the
most honest, courageous, outspoken, and ag-
gressive champion of the principles and doc-
trines that it held dear that American journalism has ever presented.

To an Evening World *staff writer falls the
assignment to tell the story of an ominous
event presaging the fall of the* World. *It was
the last staff dinner of the* Evening World.

THE LAST SUPPER

By Richard Montague

Evening World *Rewrite Man*

ON SATURDAY evening, February 21st, the
employees of the *Evening World* gathered in the Colonial Room of the Hotel Mc-
Alpin for their annual dinner, an affair at
which they were accustomed to get pleasantly
drunk, renew old acquaintances, and slap one
another on the back in the general satisfac-
tion of being employees of the *Evening World*.

At the annual dinner the rewrite man could
meet the district reporters with whom he had
conversed daily on the telephone but had not
seen since the last dinner. The compositor,
awkward in his best clothes, could mix with
editors on terms approaching equality. And
obscure employees in all departments of the

paper could, after their chiefs had absorbed sufficient liquor, address such worthies by their first names and later tell admiring wives that they had done so.

In addition to these pleasures there was the *Evening Whirl*, the annual burlesque newspaper, in which one could be almost sure to see one's name or one's picture, often coupled with that of an important executive. In short, the annual dinner of the *Evening World* was a jolly gathering.

The setting this year was the same as it always had been. The table with the cocktails on it was in the same corner of the room. The cocktails were the same color—a light yellow —and they smelled and tasted of bad gin, as they always did. Martin Hunter was mixing them, as usual. "Hello, kid!" he said as I came in. "Have one."

Jack Rainey, the city editor, and Stettenbenz, the assistant managing editor, were standing behind Martin, watching him mix the yellow fluid in the bowl, nodding to those who came to get drinks. Rainey tried to smile at me. He managed to show one of his gold teeth; but I thought he looked as if he was going to cry.

Men were forming in little groups all over the room, talking in low tones. There was an undercurrent of unrest and worry, and as I drifted from group to group it seemed that the center of each was a man who had heard a new rumor. Anyone who had heard a rumor, or imagined he had, could attract others around him in a few seconds. But everybody talked in undertones, as if ashamed to voice doubts.

The man next to me hailed the movie critic, who had recently come in. "What's this dope you've got, George?"

"Yes, what is it, George?"

"Well, I don't know, Dick, but it sounds pretty good to me. I just got it up at the Ritz, at a party. Drink brings out the truth in a guy, and this guy was pie-eyed."

"Well, for Christ's sake what is it?"

"Why, that the Scripps-Howard are going to take over the Morning and the Pulitzers' bankers are going to run the Evening. That's all I know, but I think it's the right dope."

"Why? Who was this guy, anyway?"

"I don't know who he was. I tried to find out, but couldn't. Some drunk guy."

"Sweet Jesus! Why do you believe everything some unknown drunk says?"

"Well, he told me something else that I know is true. That's why I believe this other. He said, 'I'm pie-eyed and I know I'm talking out of turn. But did you know—' and then he told me something about an actor that I know is true. And then he turned to me and he said, 'You're in the newspaper business, and I'll tell you this'—and then he spilled it."

"What does he mean by the Pulitzers' bankers?"

"I don't know. Maybe they've got themselves in deep."

"Well, I don't see why they'd sell the Morning to Scripps. What the hell do Scripps want of it?"

"This guy said Scripps wanted the Morning for the A. P. franchise and that preliminary papers were signed Friday. There's going to be an official announcement on March 21st."

"Maybe it wouldn't be so bad if a bank took us over. The Evening could go on, at least."

One of the district men, from whom I'd

doubtless been taking stories on the telephone for years but whom I didn't recognize, put a hand on my arm.

"What do you know?"

"I can't find out anything."

"There's bound to be some fire, with all this smoke. I guess I'll begin selling apples."

"Oh, balls! What's the use of worrying about it?"

"No use, Dick. No use at all, at all. Come on. Let's have a drink." He dragged me to the white table with the yellow glasses on it. Rainey was still standing behind it. Tall and straight and red of face, he seemed like an Indian chief looking his last on his tribe; looking hungrily and sadly on these men whom he had gathered together; looking his last upon them before they scattered again forever.

We sat down, finally. Darby was on one side of me, the wise Irishman, the witty, erudite papist with the shock of untamed wiry black hair. And George, the movie critic, sat on the other side. Everybody was seated now. Over at the head table were Rainey and Stet and old Martin Green, who always ran these parties. Old Martin who had never missed an

Evening World dinner in thirty years; or so
they said. And next to him sat his old friend,
Win Thomas, who used to be the Albany man.
He had some kind of a state publicity job now.
They sat there together, both genial and very
pink of face, the two old friends who had
worked on the paper so long.

I turned to George.

"Do you really think you've got the right
dope?"

"Well, I don't know, Dick, but it looks good
to me. I wouldn't have believed him if he
hadn't told me that other."

"Christ! what a business to be in! You work
your head off for a paper and then it's sold
under you."

"Maybe it would be a good thing for a lot
of us to be jolted out of it."

"It's not so easy to get jobs now, George."

"That's true."

"I don't know what I'd do. Maybe get a
publicity job somewhere. But that's not so
good, either, I guess. I wouldn't give so much
of a damn only I'm married."

"Yes, it's tough for a guy who's just been
married."

"I wonder what would happen if a bank took us over."

"Why, I think things would go on just as they have been. I doubt if it would make any difference to the fellows on the Evening."

In one corner a band was playing. The leader looked like a guy in the financial department, a red-faced, pudgy young fellow. He was waving his baton up and down and seemed to be working very hard. At every wave of his arm there was the beat of a drum that beat on my brain.

"Jesus! I wish they'd lay off that music for a while," I said to Bill, who had sat down on half my chair.

"Ought to be playin' the swan song," said Bill. "Swan song. Las' dinner we'll ever have."

"I wonder if it is."

"Sure it is. Las' dinner. Everybody knows it. We all know what's goin' to happen."

"Well, what is? I've heard enough rumors, God knows."

"Oh, I know. I know." A look of cunning stole over his drunken face. "He's selling us out. Selling us out. That's what."

"Well, what's he selling?"

47

"He's selling the *World* and the *Evening World* and the *Sunday World* and the building and the sidewalk in front of it and the fellows who work for it. He's selling everything he's got. 'Cause he's got to, that's why. And he don't give a damn."

"What's he want to sell the Evening for? That's making money."

"What's he want sell Evening for? 'Cause he can get his price for it. You can get your price for a winner. So he's goin' sell it and get a damn good price for it and go away and never be a newspaperman any more."

"Well, how about the Morning?"

"Scripps-Howard. They take it over and combine it with the Evening. Merge it, see? Merge it, retaining bes' features of each. Ha-ha! Morning and Evening *Worlds* now merged, retaining bes' features of each. 'Member that one? Ol' Munsey started all this."

He broke off suddenly and the sound from the band beat against the walls and the tables and the men sitting in the room. The men who were sitting there waiting, waiting. Waiting for some word from one of the influential

48

men on the paper, some assurance that they were not going to be sold like cattle.

"Tennant's not here, is he?" resumed Bill. And indeed the managing editor was not. He was in Atlantic City for the week-end—out of reach. "Look at Rainey over there. He looks happy, don't he? Like a man with a broken leg.

"Did you see him and Stet standing behind the bar this evening? They looked like they were crying. Oh, they know what's going to happen! And old Martin. I asked him when I came in tonight. I says, 'What do you hear, Martin?' And he says, 'O Jesus!' Just like that. 'O Jesus.' "

He rose unsteadily and put his hand on my shoulder to keep from swaying.

"The ol' swan song, Dick. Las' *Evening World* party in the worl'."

Some of the men were reading the *Whirl*. It seemed very dull this year, but nobody complained. It was always a thankless job getting out the *Whirl*; everybody knew that. Len Bonner had the job this year, and it was evident that his heart wasn't in his work.

"Look at Terhune," said Darby. "He gets bigger every year. Not any older, though."

The star alumnus of the paper was there this year, as usual. He'd begun on the *Evening World* and finally graduated to the popular magazines with his stories about dogs. Most of the men on the paper envied him his fame and money. Oh, he was well fixed now! Many glances turned to Albert Payson Terhune that evening—glances of men with fear in their hearts, who felt they were soon to be turned out on the streets; men who resented this big writer's prosperity and fame and yet who admired him sycophantically for his success and for his energy, which had made that success possible.

It was time for the speeches now.

Old Martin stood up and rapped for order. Bill lurched against me again. "Swan song," he mumbled. "Ought to be playin' the swan song."

"Oh, for Christ's sake, Bill, shut up!"

"It's the las' time, I tell you. Rainey's gone. So's Stet. So's Kelly, 'sistant business manager. See them anywhere? No. Gone."

That was very bad, very ominous, sneaking

off like that. So they wouldn't have to make any speeches. So they wouldn't be called on to deny what they could not deny. These ugly rumors. For they did not know. They were in the dark, they were as ignorant as Joe, the head copy boy, who had paid five dollars out of his fifteen-a-week salary to come.

And thinking of the young marster I remembered that he had not been seen around the office lately. He used to come in every day or so and sit at the table in the city room with Rainey and Stet. But not any more. He hadn't been in for a month. No, he could not face them any more. That was it. He knew. And he could not face them and not tell them what was going to happen to them and to all the others.

Old Martin was still pounding on the table, and finally the band stopped and he asked us all to stand and drink a silent toast to the men who had died since the last dinner—Dick Freyer, the sports editor, and some other fellow whose name I didn't catch. Some one nudged Martin's elbow. Oh yes, Arthur White, too. How could he have forgotten Arthur White? So we drank again out of the beer

goblets to Arthur White and wondered if he
and the others hadn't died in time. They didn't
have to worry about being sold.

Martin spoke in his thin voice. "When I
came to New York forty years ago things
weren't quite as they are now." You said it,
Martin. You bet they weren't. He realized he
had made a break. "I mean, we didn't have
prohibition then and you could go into a saloon
and get a free lunch if you wanted one. Well,
it was in one of those places where you could
get a free lunch that I met Win Thomas here.
Win's a big publicity man for the state now
and tells the Governor where to get off. But
he was on the *Evening World* for many years
and I think we ought to hear from him."

He paused. "But first I want to read you
some telegrams from those who wanted to be
here tonight but couldn't. Here's one from
Randy. You all know Randy. 'Regards to all
the boys and tell them I regret deeply that
I can't be with them tonight. You all know
why. Randy.' That one's from Randy.

"And here's another, from a man you all
know. Mr. John H. Tennant, our managing
editor."

"What's that?" some one shouts. "What's that? Was it collect?" There was a roar of laughter.

Martin stood patiently until the laughter subsided. " 'Missing my first *Evening World* dinner in twenty years,' " he read. " 'And, gosh! how I miss it! But with you in spirit . . . cherish memories of all those with whom . . . so long . . . happy associations.' " His voice trailed off and only disconnected words were audible. " 'With you . . . spirit . . . till last edition . . . gone to press.' "

There were faint, derisive cheers. Singularly unfortunate phraseology of the old man's. "Last edition gone to press." Nothing very cheerful about that.

I looked around the ornate room. The Colonial Room. Those heavy chandeliers must be Colonial. All hotels have to have at least one Colonial room. There were only a few men left now. All the executives and higher-ups were gone. Those who remained were underlings. And as I looked at them they seemed like children on the verge of tears—little children staying miserably on, as if they thought that merely staying on would make their dinner a joyful one; as if they could, by staying on, push away the disaster that threatened them all.

Win Thomas got up, cherubic and jovial. A good speaker, Win. But nobody cared tonight.

"You fellows all know Martin Green and you all love him. And I'm going to tell you a story about him. When Martin first came to New York he came from a paper out West. And I was the guy who got him to come here. It happened, I remember ——"

My God! What did it matter! These memories of fifty years ago. Martin Green and Win Thomas and their memories of each other. Who cared tonight?

But Win went on and on, and the little company listened with strained attention. He finally laughed suddenly and sat down.

Martin was up again and talking. And suddenly he said something that brought everybody up with a jerk. "And about these rumors," he was saying, "I want to tell you that we're not going to be sold down the river. We're going to be sold up the river!"

Everybody waited, breathless.

"Up the river." The phrase still rang in my head. And now old Martin was speaking again. "We're going to be sold up the river to the *Bronx Home News*."

There was a heartless laugh, a laugh that was almost like a sob. Oh yes! Up the Bronx River. Very good. Ha-ha!

Old Martin sat down and we looked at him resentfully. Not so funny, Martin, after all. Not so God damned funny.

"I think I'll beat it," I said. "What's the use of staying around?"

Darby watched me get up. "Are you going? I guess I will, too. This is ghastly."

In the anteroom Martin Hunter was the center of a little knot of men. Harry Cunningham, the ship-news man, was there, red-faced and good-natured, with hair grown white in the service of newspapers. And a little sharp-faced court man whose eyes were glazed from drink. And a big compositor, stolid and grave and also slightly drunk. "I don't worryin'," he kept saying. "I don't worryin'."

"What's use kiddin' yourself?" Jimmy was demanding. "What's use kiddin' yourself? You'll wake up without a job some day.

"Throw me out that's been with the paper eighteen years? It's lousy, that's what. Lousy. Eighteen years I been with this paper. And there's Bill there, thirty-four years. Going to throw men out that have been here that long? Hunh?"

"Say, when you're on a newspaper you only know you're working from pay day to pay day," said Harry. "That's all. If you get two pay days you're ahead of the game. Then you can take a vacation."

"I don't worryin'," said the compositor. "You worryin', Martin?"

"Me? No. What's the use worrying. Nobody knows a God damn thing."

"That's it. Nobody knows God damn thing. Not a God damn thing. I don't worryin'. Not God damn bit."

"I was on the *Herald* and that folded up. I was on the *Post* and that folded. Now I'm on the *Evening World*," said Harry.

"What's the use worrying?" said Martin. "Nobody knows a God damn thing."

The compositor took it up again. "Not God damn thing. Eh, Martin?"

"I was on the *Globe* just before it folded,"

said Harry. "That's one I missed. So I'm ahead of the game."

"I don't worryin'," said the compositor. "Nah!"

I went out to the checkroom where one of the radio men was flirting with the girl, taking the dummy quarters out of the saucer. "Come on, big boy, give 'em back. If the boss comes along and sees you he'll give my job back to me."

Give my job back. Christ, everything goes back to that.

Another old reporter who had worn himself out in the service of the paper was fumbling in his pocket for his hat check. "I've lost it," he mumbled. "I've lost it."

"Oh, no you haven't," said the girl. A pretty girl. Too bad if she should lose her job.

"Look in your pocket, old man," I said. "Maybe it's in your pocket."

"Oh no. No. Not in my pocket. Not nothing in my pocket. Nothing in the world."

He produced the check from his pocket.

"See?" said the girl. "I knew you had it."

"It was in my pocket," he said.

I got my coat and went out. In the elevator I saw one of the sports writers. "Nice evening, eh?"

"Jesus!" he said.

"I think I'll go up and see if there are any jobs loose on the *Times*."

On Washington's birthday the rumors of the World's *end had become news, and a reporter had to be assigned the task of finding out if his own paper was to be sold.*

THE *WORLD* FOR SALE

By A. A. Schechter

Reporter, the World

HAD Surrogate James A. Foley remained home on Washington's Birthday instead of playing golf at the Winged Foot club in Westchester, the *World* would have "scooped" the town on its own sale and demise.

But it was a holiday and Surrogate Foley likes to play golf, so here goes a new lead.

This department (I understand all columnists and journalists refer to themselves that way) was given the first assignment on the proposed sale of the *World* papers.

We had just finished a piece of rewrite sent in by a publicity office when James W. Barrett, the city editor, called us to the desk and asked if an assignment could be kept in the strictest confidence by us until we discovered the veracity or falseness of the story.

We agreed, and into our laps was thrown the assignment, "find out if the *World* is to be sold."

And right at this point (as long as we have several thousand words to write) we might tell those up and coming journalists, who at some time or other may have to cross their own publishers' paths, that it's ticklish, funny, unusual, creepy business. It's like going out with your best friend's wife.

But to get back to our original theme song.

Unabashed, stalwart, or whatever you want to call it, we marched through the little iron gate, right into the foyer and stoutly pressed the door bell of the Foley abode.

A young woman, whom later we found to be very helpful in the quest for information, notified us that Surrogate Foley was golfing.

"He always goes to Westchester with his friends when court is closed," we were told.

And then we started in.

If we could only record what we told her, tears would bespatter this page. There is no written record of what the Foley homestead listened to from eight o'clock to midnight, but we are sure that a graphic picture of unemployed men, pawning typewriters, and police cards must have impressed itself on the mind of that kind young lady.

The next appearance at the Foley homestead took place at eight o'clock Tuesday morning, February 24th, and there, just six hours before anyone else learned about it, we were told that "the Pulitzer matter comes up at four o'clock in open chambers at the Hall of Records."

Still, being a reporter, we hopped another taxicab and rushed to the office, only to be greeted with a "what the hell are you doing so early?"

We were on a confidential assignment, however, and told no one until Mr. Barrett had arrived at the office.

Together we rushed—no, that's wrong. *World* elevators creep—to the twelfth floor, where we started to discuss some system of getting down to earth on the story.

My first assignment that bright morning of the 24th of February was to cover the assign-

ment in routine fashion at Surrogate's Court.
Later we wrote it with Philip Pearl, another reporter, who had later been assigned by the
desk to cover everything up to the time the
Surrogate adjourned court for the day.

Surrogate's Court is on the fifth floor of
the Hall of Records Building. It's a drab, stone
building, very gloomy and internally lofty.
The judges are so carefully guarded that to
see them elsewhere but on the bench is considered a miracle.

We are sure that the elevator operators in
the Hall of Records knew the *World* was to
be sold three days before the decision was
handed down, for no longer did a working
member of the press receive any homage or
respect from them.

It may have been that we were sleepy after
the long vigil at the Foley homestead, but anyway we moved too slowly for the elevator man
and were told to "wake up."

The rectangular corridors on the fifth floor
were teeming with reporters, excitement, more
reporters, photographers, and a dozen or more
self-styled publishers' representatives and
lawyers.

At least a dozen well-dressed scribes were mistaken for the Pulitzer brothers, and finally we were pressed into service by photographers to assist in identifying the *Worlds'* owners. We agreed to assist.

Several reporters from the *Evening Telegram* were there, too. They knew all about the story. In fact, it was all set up in type, we were informed, but, of course, Roy Howard had asked them to keep it in the strictest of confidence.

There was Ishbel Ross, the competent and very pretty woman reporter from the *Herald Tribune*. She too, she told us, knew all about the *World* sales, and her office, too, had the story in type. No, she couldn't tell us any more about it.

Thirty minutes after our arrival in Surrogate's Court, Joseph Brady, *Evening World* reporter assigned to the story with us, was in a deep huddle to determine our course of action.

Right then and there we decided that all the other newspapermen were a "God damned bunch of ———— ————" for not letting us in on the inside of the story. It may sound dubious, but the *World* staff knew less about the proposed sale of its paper than any other newspaper in town.

Still alert in the corridors, we heard about the *Telegram* installing new wires; the *Telegram* ready to scrap the *Worlds* immediately after the decision; of an extra night crew of mechanical forces ordered to report to the *Telegram* Building; of the new *World-Telegram* masthead lying that moment on Roy Howard's desk. We heard hundreds of rumors, all of which eventually came true, much to our chagrin.

We had a great time before court convened. We displayed our advance order, a pink slip whereby we drew an advance on our salary for expenses. We approached the *Telegram* scribes with a serious demeanor, and asked them if they deemed it advisable for me to rush back to The World Building and draw cash for Barrett's still authoratative signature. Everyone laughed at this. We wished now we had several dozen pink slips.

Finally at five o'clock Surrogate Foley ascended the bench and seventy newsgatherers, publishers, and court loungers arose to pay judicial respects to the man who finally was to allow the sale of the papers.

Roy Howard, the dapper little publisher of a coast-to-coast chain of newspapers, entered with his son. The three Pulitzers entered with their staff of attorneys, headed by John G. Jackson, the first of a long line of attorneys who finally construed the thought of the Joseph Pulitzer will so as to allow the sale of the newspapers.

Max D. Steuer sauntered in. A hubbub, a craning of heads, and a buzz through the courtroom. No one knew why or for whom he was there.

"Your Honor, please," said Counseler Steuer, "I represent Paul Block, and he is on his way from the coast to bid on the *World* newspapers." Newspapers, he explained, for which Block had bid far in excess of the $5,-000,000 price set by Roy Howard and the Scripps-Howard Alliance.

The astute Mr. Jackson, representing the Pulitzers, appeared much surprised and agitated by the appearance of outside interests in halting the expected rushing through of the *World* sale.

It was a pathetic scene.

There on the stand Herbert Pulitzer, youngest and chief heir of the Pulitzer sons, confessed his inability to make the Press Publishing papers pay for themselves.

His expected few minutes on the stand were made more and more embarrassing by the prying questions of Vincent L. Leibell and Thomas I. Sheridan, attorneys for the infant heirs of the later Joseph Pulitzer. They were court appointees. They could ask all and as many pointed and flustering questions as they pleased, and they did. Especially questions about intangible assets.

The proceedings continued and continued. We looked out of the window in Surrogate Foley's chambers and saw the Pulitzer Building. Immediately we thought of a lead to use on the story for the next morning. Something about having the papers sold from a courtroom where the windows looked upon the gold dome. We noticed, too, for the first time, that the gold dome had turned green. Something that may have taken place a year before, but hitherto unnoticed.

And suddenly the courtroom sat up tense again.

Herbert Pulitzer was on the stand, his hand covering his mouth, answering in a low, modulated voice.

To the best of our recollection, as our notes have since been thrown away, his answers were something to this effect:

Mr. Leibell: "Mr. Pulitzer, what is the annual rental of the Pulitzer Building?"

Mr. Pulitzer: "I couldn't say, offhand. Mr. Van Benthuysen [the treasurer of the *World*] can answer that."

Mr. Leibell: "How much space does the *World* occupy in the building?"

Mr. Pulitzer: "I'm not sure, I think about half, but Mr. Van Benthuysen has the papers with him."

Several more such questions and unsatisfactory answers followed, and Surrogate Foley interjected, "Mr. Leibell, why don't you recall Mr. Van Benthuysen to the stand if you want the answers to those questions?"

Mr. Van Benthuysen was recalled.

And so it continued until almost eight o'clock, with Surrogate Foley reserving de-

cision despite the warnings of Roy Howard
and Attorney Jackson that a twenty-four-hour
delay would wreck the *World* papers.

Said Roy Howard: "Your Honor, a layman
cannot appreciate the fact, but it is clear to
see that the morale of the *World* staff is
wrecked. The proposed sale of the papers will
wreck its circulation and advertising overnight. People will not buy a dying newspaper.
They will not advertise in it."

His own newspaper, Mr. Howard told the
court, would of course benefit materially by
the delay. Everyone would jump on the band-
wagon.

Mr. Jackson, the Pulitzers' attorney, continued: "A delay of twenty-four hours on the
decision would wreck the *World*. Its circulation would fall. Its force would be too demoral-
ized to continue publication."

Herbert Pulitzer's final parting words: "The
World cannot be successful because it is in a
class midway between the high-type newspapers like the *Times, Herald Tribune* and the
Sun, and the tabloids on the other side."

Surrogate Foley reserved decision, however, and as you will find in the succeeding

chapters, the *Worlds* lived a glorious life for the next three days.

Despite the warnings of Messrs. Howard and Jackson, circulation did not drop. It gained 8,000 the next day. Advertising increased. The paper jumped from twenty-six pages to twenty-eight to carry the additional advertising. The *Evening World* did likewise.

The morale of the *World* staff was not wrecked that night, nor on the next two nights. To the very end, it remained a loyal, enterprising gang of newspapermen, bent on turning out a perfect newspaper and watching out for libels.

It was this morale which caused Ralph E. Renaud, the managing editor, to remark for the first time since his advent on the *World*, that, "by God! there are men on the *World*."

The former managing editor of a Philadelphia newspaper records here what took place on the second day of the World's *sale proceedings.*

ENTER DON QUIXOTES

By John T. Gibbs

AND then there rode upon the scene several hundred Don Quixotes, of whom I was an obscure one.

They set out to save the *World*. There was something fantastically unreal about them, something a little absurd. In twelve hours they wrote into the history of American journalism a chapter on almost heroic futility. Their effort excited world-wide notice for a day or so and then was forgotten in the march of events.

Wednesday, February 25th, was their single day of glory. This was the day which began with vague hope and ended in a blaze of enthusiasm. This was the day on which many of the 3,000 Pulitzer employees tried to buy the *World* newspapers for themselves.

70

Three thousand men and women suddenly faced the loss of their jobs. The threat came at a time when the city, the nation, and the world were filled to desperation with unemployed, when places were peculiarly hard to get, when gigantic efforts to relieve the distress of the idle were proving only partly successful.

Dread of the bread line undoubtedly lurked in the recesses of many minds among us that day, but I doubt if this dread motivated the extraordinary demonstrations which began at noon and reached the climax at midnight. Something more than mere jobs was at stake. Most of the 3,000 sensed somehow that they were part of an institution which had a definite and important function in the American cosmos.

Overnight this institution had been threatened with extinction. Had it vanished instantly, as well it might had not the Paul Block offer intervened, they would have accepted the fact as one accepts an earthquake. But it had not been annihilated. This morning the *World* had come out as usual.

The 3,000 were in the position of a pugilist who finds himself still on his feet with

his guard up after receiving on the point of
the chin what was intended to be a knockout
punch. The blow had been delivered, but
there was the *World* still being published. In
this fact glowed a spark of hope.

Optimism guided the gossip of the groups
around the *World* office who discussed the
situation. Paul Block's offer surely would prevent the sale to Scripps-Howard. The appearance of the busy Max Steuer had its significance; political factors were interested, it
was whispered. Mighty names were mentioned
as probable backers of Block or as independent bidders. There was to be another hearing
before the Surrogate today, at which the
scheme to sell and junk all the *World* papers
would be thwarted.

These were not slaves speculating on the
auction block as to the identity of their new
masters. The men and women of the *World*
were impatient. In the minds of each rose the
question: What can I do, I, personally? Only
a leader was needed to offer some definite
suggestion.

This leader appeared in the person of James
W. Barrett, city editor of the morning *World*.

MR. BARRETT AT HIS LATE DESK

His suggestion was, "Let's buy the *World* ourselves."

Such a program bristled with spikes and spines. A thousand arguments could be offered against it; a hundred unanswerable questions arose. Where could we, even 3,000 of us, get the money?

Objections were brushed aside or argued down. Few indeed were even uttered, although undoubtedly most of us entered upon this venture with mental reservations, aware of its wild improbability, but rather expecting some miracle to transpire which would make all caution seem petty.

I was lifted out of my morning sleep by a telephone call from the *World* office, instructing me to cover the Surrogate's hearing on the *World* case, scheduled for 11 A.M. On reaching the Hall of Records, I learned that the hearing had been postponed until one o'clock, so I wandered over to the *World* office.

Ordinarily at noon the editorial office of a morning newspaper contains only a few men, but this day there was a sizable crowd present. As yet the idea had not been born, but Barrett was at his desk, busy with telephone calls.

The first intimation I had of the Barrett plan was when Abe Schechter said to me, "If the employees could get together, they might hold up the sale, Barrett says."

I went up to his desk. He was saying: "I have got a lawyer who thinks we might delay this thing. He's willing to give his services free if we are willing to authorize him. We have to get at least twenty persons to sign an authorization to him to go ahead."

"What's the Idea?" I asked.

"We will ask the Surrogate to hold up his decision until the employees can make the Pulitzers an offer to buy the paper themselves. I have no idea how many will want to go in or what outside money we can get, but if the Surrogate will give us a little time, we can at least make the attempt. That's all our lawyer will ask."

Almost instantly a paper giving Gustavus A. Rogers the right to appear as attorney for *World* employees was drawn up. Schechter, Phil Pearl, and George Hall made copies and laid them on Barrett's desk.

"I am warning all those who sign this," said Barrett, "that it might get them in wrong with the Pulitzers, and perhaps with Roy Howard, too. Maybe they'll find they've attached their names to a blacklist."

Whereupon Barrett signed his name first. Half a dozen of us signed directly under his name immediately. Several went over to the *Evening World* office to get more signatures, while some one else got up a list of pledges of money for the purchase of the newspapers. Things boomed from the first moment.

One o'clock neared and we all had to go over to the Surrogate's court. Barrett took the first sheet of the authorization with him, while several volunteers remained in the office to get more signatures, which were relayed to the courtroom.

I might note at this point that it was a beautiful late winter day, clear and snappy but not cold. As we walked over to the Hall of Records, the absurd thought occurred to me that no catastrophe affecting 3,000 persons directly and hundreds of thousands of readers indirectly could happen on a day like this.

The corridors outside the Surrogate's hearing-room were jammed, mostly with reporters from other papers. We all marched directly into the courtroom, while Barrett met Attorney Rogers. There we sat for half an hour until Surrogate Foley appeared on the bench. The seats were filled with *World* employees.

At the long table in front of the bench Barrett and our attorney were first to seat themselves. Other lawyers and litigants entering from time to time looked curiously at them, perhaps wondering what they were doing there, as the news of the employees' action had not yet spread abroad.

The attorneys for the Pulitzers and the infant heirs came in, then Roy Howard and his counsel, then Paul Block with Max Steuer, all of whom sat at the counsel table. The three Pulitzers, however, did not seat themselves with their lawyers, but occupied places in the front row of the side seats to the left, Ralph in the middle, Joseph on his right, and Herbert on his left. They exchanged a word or two with one another but with no one else, not even their attorneys.

Paul Block was in earnest discussion with Max Steuer, but appeared calm. Roy Howard was animated, exchanging bows with acquaintances in the courtroom, waving his hands and smiling. The Pulitzers sat like three stone images, while we all waited.

The *World* reporter who sat next to me stared at the Pulitzers and swore to me that neither Ralph nor Joseph ever looked in our direction, although Herbert occasionally stole a glance at us, quickly averting his eyes when he found any of us looking at him.

Our group of twelve or fifteen *World* reporters mostly discussed Barrett. It was daring of him, while still a Pulitzer employee, to appear thus boldly in court opposing their wishes. We admired his action and swore to stick by him if it could do him any good. Still we waited.

A man entered the courtroom, carrying an armload of *Evening Worlds*, which he distributed free. It was a most uncourtroom-like procedure, but the attendants apparently couldn't make up their minds whether to stop him or not. On the first page of this edition was a two-column box, which spread the information in bold type that the advertising and circulation of both the morning and evening *Worlds* were showing gains.

The three Pulitzers read this and buzzed

among themselves. A man came up to Herbert and he spoke to him, whereupon the man left the courtroom. I learned later that Herbert had ordered this box removed from later editions. Some one in the *Evening World* office had taken a direct slap at his employers in their own paper. They were asking to sell and scrap the papers because they were losing money. Here was an obstinate employee virtually denying their contention. I do not know who did this or who sent the newsman into the courtroom, but it was a bold strike of independence almost equal to Barrett's.

At long length, Surrogate Foley entered and took his seat on the bench. He announced at once that the attorneys had agreed to a private conference, but before he could call them into consultation, Attorney Rogers intervened and sprang the bombshell of the employees' intervention.

Of course, his action did not surprise us, but it probably shook the Pulitzers, and perhaps even Howard and Block. The Surrogate himself listened patiently to Mr. Rogers' plea. The attorney asked that decision be delayed to give the employees a chance to make an offer. He cited the figures given by the freely-distributed copy of the *Evening World* to show that undue emphasis had been placed by the Pulitzers in their original application upon the losses borne by the newspaper properties. He even hinted that these losses were exaggerated. He pointed out that Joseph Pulitzer desired above all else to have the *World* continue, and said that, if his sons did not desire to bear the burden of continuing these institutions, at least the law should not permit them to be extinguished entirely, but should allow them to be continued by those willing to carry on, and who could do this more appropriately than the very men and women who were now getting them out each day? Mr. Rogers admitted the employees had no definite plan of purchase, but said this was not to be wondered at, because they had been given no time. He promised, however, that the employees, if given ten days by the Surrogate, would come forward with an offer at least as good as that made by Scripps-Howard, and with the added feature of carrying out the expressed will of Joseph Pulitzer to keep these newspapers alive.

Finally Mr. Rogers begged the Surrogate to allow Mr. Barrett to take the stand and explain what had been done in a few hours by the employees toward raising a fund to buy the papers. The Surrogate ignored this request, but immediately called all the attorneys into conference about his bench, admitting Mr. Rogers to this discussion.

For two hours the lawyers stood there and talked. What they said I do not know, as it was a private consultation of attorneys. Their clients were not with them. The three Pulitzers sat together, more silent than ever, and waited. Roy Howard and Paul Block went off in a corner and talked together for half an hour. Their conference looked ominous to us and probably was a forecast of the withdrawal of the Block offer the next day. Howard then resumed his seat and began reading his own newspaper, the *Telegram*.

The knot of lawyers around the Surrogate's bench talked and talked. Even today I cannot imagine what they talked about. Probably they were discussing the points of law involved. The Surrogate was considering a variety of questions. The first was the breaking of Joseph Pulitzer's will, in which he instructed his sons to carry on his newspapers regardless of profits. The sons had pleaded to sell the newspapers because they were losing money and impairing the estate. A second point was the plea of Paul Block that the proposed sale of the papers to Scripps-Howard be halted because he had made a better offer. Still a third point was the application of the employees. And, there was also the objections raised by the attorneys for the infant heirs.

At any rate, when the conference ended, the Surrogate did not announce his decision, but stated that no ruling would be made until eleven o'clock the following morning at the earliest.

To us that meant another day's delay; that much more time to formulate plans for buying the newspapers. It was the second gleam of hope and it was the occasion for the remarkable demonstration of that evening.

Out in the hallway, after the hearing, Max Steuer said: "I am authorized by Mr. Block to say that, if his offer is accepted, he will give the employees of the *World* not ten days but thirty days in which to take the paper off his hands at the same price he pays for it. He wants no profit, not even my fee."

That sounded extraordinarily generous of Mr. Block, and the employees who heard Mr. Steuer were still further cheered by this announcement.

Looking back, I wonder what it meant. The next day Mr. Block withdrew his offer of purchase, saying he had not understood that the Pulitzers had already entered into a contract to sell to Scripps-Howard. Both these statements had a strange flavor. Before making his offer to the *World* employees, Mr. Block had talked with Mr. Steuer and had held a half-hour conference with Mr. Howard. Is it possible that he had not learned in these two long conferences that a contract existed between the Pulitzers and Howard? Or had he not read the morning papers, in which this contract was explained? And, if he knew there was a contract which would cause his withdrawal as a bidder the next day, why did he raise the false hopes of the *World* employees by making his apparently generous offer to them? This is one of the enigmas of the situation.

It was now late in the afternoon. We all returned to the *World* office. We were then given a pleasant surprise. In the first place, all the New York afternoon papers were filled with the story of the attempt of the *World* employees to buy the papers. Barrett was suddenly hailed as a newspaper hero. Also, there began to pour into Barrett's desk offers of financial aid from all parts of the city and all sections of the United States.

Up to that time the purchase plans had been nebulous. Almost at once they became concrete. Again Barrett had an idea—he would call together a meeting of *World* employees that very night. Hurriedly it was arranged with the Hotel Astor to place a meeting-room at our disposal. Notices were typewritten and sent to all departments, asking employees to attend. It was after 5:30 before these notices were posted. Many of the business-office workers and *Evening World* employees had gone home for the day. Many of the morning *World* workers would be at work at the time set for the meeting, 9:30 P.M.

"If we get a hundred, we'll be lucky," said Barrett, "but it will give us a start."

I would have attended the meeting anyhow, but I was assigned to cover it also. In the interval between the Surrogate's hearing and the night meeting, while I was writing my afternoon story, there were all sorts of activity around the *World* office. People from all departments crowded the city room. Outsiders poured in and stood about, gazing at us curiously. Reporters from other newspapers used our telephones and sat on our desks.

Meanwhile, as always through these three last days, the routine of the office went on. There was no slowing down by the night desk, the copy desk, the sports writers, or anyone else. Men were sent out on assignments, each one probably the last they would cover for the *World*, and covered them with fervor. I have heard of other newspapers dying or sold, on which the men let things slide in the last few days, broke up furniture like legislatures on the last day of a session, or went off on howling sprees. On that second day there was not a single drunken reporter on the morning *World*—not one. Even on the last day, if I may go beyond the topic assigned me in this book, there were only a few who even took a

84

drink up until the last edition on the last night
went to press.

With one mind, everybody seemed deter-
mined to stick it out to the end, getting out the
best newspaper possible even if it was to be
the last ever sent out of that shop. On this
second day, of course, we were buoyed up by
the hope that the *World* would continue and
that we would own it, but this was not the
spirit which animated the workers on the first
day, nor had it anything to do with the dogged
perseverance of those who got out the final
editions on the third day after all hope had
fled.

Telephones were busy early that evening of
the second day. Those who had not seen the
notice of the night meeting were informed at
their homes that the employees were to gather
at the Astor. Even at that, nobody anticipated
the size of the turnout.

I went home to dinner and did not get there
until 9:30. As soon as I entered the hallway
of the ninth floor, where the meeting was held,
I was amazed at the crowd. Fully 200 persons
were standing about, men and women from
every department of the Morning, Evening

and Sunday *Worlds*. Seldom have I witnessed such enthusiasm. It was as if the victory was at the point of being won. More employees were pouring in, and when the meeting finally opened at ten o'clock, 450 persons were jammed into the hall.

The climax of the day was reached in that hall. George Hall opened the meeting by praising Barrett and then turned the gavel over to the city editor, who spoke briefly on the purpose of the meeting. All the fear of the morning had vanished. There was no talk of blacklisting or of the danger being run by the intervening employees. The publicity and the response from all parts of the country had eliminated that.

Barrett said we were assembled to carry out the wishes of Joseph Pulitzer, wishes which were being ignored. He spoke glowingly of the opportunities of building up a unique employee-owned group of newspapers. Then he began reading messages of encouragement. From bankers came offers of financial assistance. From men on other newspapers came subscriptions. From the Paris and Chicago bureaus of the *World* came large donations.

From the staffs of newspapers in far-off corners of the country came offers of aid.

It had been announced before the meeting that *World* employees themselves had pledged $750,000. Before the night was over this sum was swollen by offers from the hall and from outside sources to $1,500,000. All America seemed aroused over the danger of losing its leading liberal newspapers. A ground swell seemed to be setting in which would force Roy Howard and the Pulitzers to abandon their efforts to junk the papers; it appeared as if public sentiment was making itself heard.

At least that's how it seemed to those of us in the hall. "Now they will not dare to scrap the *World*," was even uttered in enthusiasm.

The *World* employes cheered almost every utterance of Barrett. Likewise they gave a rousing hand to Attorney Rogers, who spoke after the city editor, telling of the legal difficulties in the path of the project, but declaring that all these would disappear if this sort of enthusiasm was continued. Mr. Rogers said he had discovered some things in Mr. Pulitzer's will which might further hold up the agreement of sale. Everybody was filled with confidence.

Mr. Barrett was made permanent president of The World Employees Coöperative Association. The meeting got down to business at the suggestion of the chair by dividing into groups according to departments and electing delegates to a central committee, which was to formulate a program. This committee was quickly chosen and retired to the hallway to deliberate. While it was out, the chairman continued reading telegrams and messages of encouragement.

The committee came back with its resolutions empowering Mr. Barrett to continue to receive pledges and Mr. Rogers to pursue his legal objections to the sale of the papers. Then the meeting adjourned. The Don Quixotes lingered for a few minutes to talk it over enthusiastically, then went away, never to meet again. It was a few minutes after midnight, and the day of enthusiasm and hope was over; the breathing-space between the delivery of the first thrust and the crash of the death blow had come to an end.

Few of us knew it. We went home filled with

the belief we had started a new era in American journalism. With several others of the Morning *World* staff I went down to the office. There we found the executives, desk men, and rewrite men working as usual. We told them about the meeting and they were properly impressed. Perhaps we even communicated some of our enthusiasm to them. We lingered late, talking. We hesitatingly murmured our doubts, but mainly expressed our hopes. We were nearly convinced that the *World* had been saved.

Now, I do not desire to anticipate the words of those assigned to write about the third day or to sum up the last days of the *World*, but I would like to say here and now that it was a crying shame to see all this fervor wasted. There existed among a great majority of the 450 in the Hotel Astor that night of February 25, 1931, something which might have resulted in a splendid coöperative newspaper enterprise had not Surrogate Foley, twenty-four hours later, decided to judge the case before him strictly on its legal merits. I think the *World*, as it appeared from day to day, showed a caliber of employee putting it together a little

different from that of the ordinary newspaper
—perhaps a little better. I think a group of in-
dividuals had been gotten together over a long
period of years peculiarly fitted to do all the little tasks which contribute to the making of a
great liberal newspaper, and that gaps in this
group had been filled from time to time by persons who fitted into its general scheme. I think
this group displayed its spirit in following
where Barrett led. In this group there was the
will to act coöperatively and the ability to
make that coöperation successful. Both the
will and the ability were wasted when the
World died.

It is pleasant to think of what might have
been. Calmly judging events in after-time, one
sees the almost insurmountable difficulties in
the way of employee ownership of a newspaper,
but after all, American annals are filled with
successes whose beginnings were even more
dubious.

"Published as usual" was the notice from *Herbert Pulitzer to the* World *staff while awaiting the court's decision, so they turned out 400,000 copies of the March 1* Sunday World *which never reached the newsstands.*

THE HELL-BOX EDITION OF THE *SUNDAY WORLD*

By Herman Michelson

Sunday Editor

Last December, in response to a request from R. H. Lyman, editor of the World Almanac, for a résumé of the *Sunday World's* past year, to be included in the Almanac's annual history of the paper, I dictated, to a puzzled and incredulous secretary, the following:

"The progress of the *Sunday World* in 1930 was notable for consistency in one direction. During January a decisive step was taken in killing the Second News Section. After getting rid of such readers as might be interested in the development of the background of the week's news, an even-handed

91

justice dictated that the Sunday Magazine readers be weeded out. Accordingly, an inferior quality of paper was substituted for the Magazine. This embraced a further possible economy in that color reproductions became so bad that one picture might have been used several times, with different captions, and no one be the wiser. The size of the Magazine was cut successively to twenty, to sixteen, and finally to twelve pages.

"The hoped-for result seemed in sight when the summer slump in circulation developed huge proportions. To discourage those who might have sought to buy the paper on returning to the city in early fall, the usual departments, drama, books, art, music, were held down to microscopic size. But the habit of reading a certain paper, once implanted, has a pernicious virility of its own, and it presently became apparent that circulation was picking up. Then the management played its trump card. In October, Herbert Pulitzer persuaded the *Times* and *Herald Tribune* to join with him in raising the price of the Sunday paper to ten cents. He was rewarded by seeing the *Sunday World's* circulation, which was around 500,000 and climbing in October, drop 135,000 in six weeks."

Having relieved my mind in this wise, I got together another piece, in quite a different vein, and turned it in to the Almanac, where it duly appeared. That was in December.

In February there are premonitory rumblings for the *Sunday World*. A week or so before the end a new and unworkable policy is instituted—payment on publication only. With characteristic abruptness the new system is first proclaimed at the cashier's window. Several writers—vacation-bound and in need of funds—present vouchers for accepted Sunday stories, and are turned away. Half an hour later the Sunday editor gets his first notice that such vouchers are not to be issued.

Next comes a portentous memorandum from the treasurer's office about "certain paintings" which the Sunday department has scheduled for publication. The treasurer feels —and the general manager feels with him— that these should be safeguarded. Bob Ament, art director, descends on a mission of inquiry, and shortly staggers back upstairs, overcome. It is pointed out to him that on the list of material on hand there are certain items which are too valuable to be left about. The Magazine has been running a weekly page of reproductions from the masters, aimed at the high-school art-study classes. "Here—and here—Rembrandt—Van Dyke—Rubens. . . . These must be very valuable old paintings!"

A portent of approaching events, and possibly a clue to the mental processes of the powers that be.

First official notice comes Tuesday afternoon from R. E. Renaud, managing editor: ". . . unpleasant news . . . to be sold this afternoon to the *Telegram* . . . in all probability tomorrow last issue of the *World* . . . no *Sunday World*." And throws out the newswise reflection, "Wouldn't it be a curious thing if the Surrogate refused to let 'em sell?"

Back to the Magazine, where Ament awaits word. Bill Randorf, assistant Sunday editor, is dictating to Mary Davis, rejections, acceptances, ideas on how to improve stories—an interminable series. Ten minutes beforehand, with dire tidings, Ament and I sit behind his oblivious back and listen as he arranges for issues that never will roll from the press, and

cackle with acrid mirth. Finally Randorf finishes, swings round—and learns that he has
just ploughed a neat straight furrow in the sea.

The news has spread in the feature department, upstairs. Mrs. Patience Cole, in charge
of the Biggest News of the Week contest, and
Miss Dorothy Alford, secretary to the department and doubling in brass as reader of the
essays, are snowed under. The high schools
have chosen this week to roll up a record—
more than 2,000 essays—and the two ladies
are surrounded, overtopped, almost hidden by
the piles. They gaze out from the mess ap-
pealingly. Shall they go on reading, judging,
awarding? ". . . in all probability . . . but
if Surrogate Foley should refuse? . . ." Better wade through the pile as usual; there may
be a Sunday paper yet. The work goes on.

Wednesday: An important story is late—
Elliot Thurston's from Washington, on Hoover's second year. A wire finds him and he re-
sponds: "Thought you wouldn't want it. Filing two thousand tonight." The first page of
the Editorial Section is laid out to feature his
story; Leo Kober starts on a picture. Joe Liebling reports on the first large-scale public dem-

onstration of the rumba, sultriest of the newer dances, and this is scheduled for the Metropolitan Section. Herb Roth draws the job of illustrating it. Sylvia Lewis, Women's Section editor, produces a perfectly grand story, the answer to any editor's prayer—it's news, it's sensational, it's a hundred per cent woman stuff, and it carries a power interest for men. Dictator Machado has been emptying Cuba's jails of their toughest female characters, and turning them loose to assault women nationalists in the streets, to tear their clothes from them and set them out in the full blaze of Havana's squares, naked. This goes into type as the lead story in her section, with a streamer headline.

Meanwhile, the question, Is there to be a Sunday paper? The managing editor doesn't know; nobody knows. Eventually a Pulitzer bulletin appears: pending the court's decision the morning, evening and Sunday editions will be "published as usual."

The Rotogravure Section goes to press on time. Half the edition of next Sunday's Magazine, which was put on the color presses last Saturday, is printed now, and by Friday morn-

ing the whole edition is off and distributed
to the newsdealers. Technically the March 1
issue of the Magazine is never published. Actually many copies find their way into news-
boys' hands and sell at a premium. The last
edition of the poor old starved Rotogravure is
simply scrapped.

Patience Cole reports that a Jacob Weis-
berg of New Utrecht High School has won the
Biggest News contest and a twenty-dollar
prize. Modified rapture for Jake. Let him not
hope to collect!

Thursday: The paper begins to assume its
final shape. Herb Roth finishes his portrayal
of the rumba. Leo Kober does a cubistic
Hoover that spells trouble fore and aft. Thurston's story arrives and goes to the printers. An
error is discovered in the advance proofs of
a late March issue of the Magazine, and the
neogravure plant uptown is halted in mid-
career to correct it. Fashion writers, sketch artists, literary agents, free-lance writers, come
and go. In the midst of it all there drifts in
the supreme optimist, a young man in search
of a job. Editing of copy goes on until eight-
thirty at night, after which there remains only

that extraordinary death watch in the city room.

Friday: In the composing-room they are pulling out the galleys of type and dumping them into the hell-box.

Ordinarily the man on the assignment desk is seen and heard but not read; in this case his narrative is an essential and compelling part of the picture.

THE LAST DAY

By Alex Schlosser

Acting Day City Editor

THE last day of the *World* began after a hectic night. Every man and woman on the staff of the paper, from the press-room to the Dome, felt instinctively that the great paper soon was to be gathered to its fathers, despite the valiant last-minute fight to save it.

Throughout that last day, and far into the night, they waited tensely for announcement from the Surrogate's Court heralding the doom of the institution which Joseph Pulitzer had established nearly fifty years before. The same institution, it should be remarked, that Mr. Pulitzer regarded, at the time of his sudden death in 1911, as an indestructible, imperishable, almost immortal monument to his memory.

The night before had witnessed scenes unique in the history of American journalism. As elsewhere described, six hundred employees of the paper gathered at the Hotel Astor, under the leadership of James W. Barrett, city editor, to fight for the preservation of Joseph Pulitzer's "imperishable" monument and, incidentally, almost quite incidentally, one would judge, for the protection of their own jobs.

The night was long and tense. Probably never before in this country did any journalistic staff meet for such a purpose, animated by the same startling, spontaneous impulse. They were there for nothing less than to frustrate the plans of their employers, Ralph, Joseph, and Herbert Pulitzer, to sell the paper to the Scripps-Howard organization. If they could, they would buy the paper from the Pulitzers to perpetuate the great founder's ideals by running it themselves.

Others have told about this meeting and its surprising issue. The part assigned to me in this little history is to recount the actions and reactions of the mournful day that followed in the editorial rooms of the *World*, which I now proceed to do:

Arrived at office about 9:30 after reading Thursday morning newspapers. *Times* and *Herald Tribune* led papers with prospective sale of *World* and gathering of employees to stop it. Noted Jim Barrett had become a national figure in journalism overnight. I was proud of him. *World* printed sale negotiations fully, but did not lead paper with story, preferring for that distinction the seizure of druggists in a rum round-up. Wondered why this was and decided it was no business of mine.

Emptied night basket containing memoranda from the night desk—letters, futures, and what not. Considered for a moment whether I should save futures in view of approaching dissolution, but habit triumphed and they were marked for proper filing and began to think of futures that had been marked for two, three, five, and ten years ahead. Wondered whether they ever would be used if Surrogate Foley authorized sale of paper.[1]

Called Mr. Barrett on phone and learned he had not reached home during night, but re-

[1] EDITOR's NOTE—We gave our futures to the *Telegram* after the sale.

mained at work in home of Gustavus Rogers, counsel for World Employees' Co-operative Association, which had been formed at Hotel Astor meeting. Knew he never could tear himself away from the cause he had undertaken and prepared to go through day's work without him.

Glanced at New York City News Association schedule. Routine assignments: "Bank of U. S. Developments. Open Hearing in Appellate Division Inquiry, etc." How could anyone be interested in such things with the paper's fate hanging in the balance? Yet they ought to be covered.

Gibbs "did" *World* sale story day before. Remembered Thursday was his day off. Phoned to ask what he was going to do. He said he would take regular day off unless office desired otherwise. Told him to do so.

Bulletin from City News:

"SURROGATES' COURT—WORLD SALE. PAUL BLOCK, OWNER OF THE 'BROOKLYN STANDARD UNION' AND OTHER NEWSPAPERS THROUGHOUT THE COUNTRY TODAY— THUR.—UNCONDITIONALLY WITHDREW THE

OFFER MADE FOR THE PURCHASE OF THE
Worlds (MORNING, SUNDAY AND EVENING)
THROUGH AN ANNOUNCEMENT MADE BY HIS
ATTORNEY, MAX D. STEUER.

"MR. BLOCK BASED HIS WITHDRAWAL ON
TWO FACTORS; THAT HE DID NOT WISH TO
OPPOSE THE EFFORTS OF THE EMPLOYEES
TO OBTAIN CONTROL OF THE PAPER AND
THAT HE DID NOT WISH TO INTERFERE WITH
THE CONCLUDED DEAL ENTERED INTO BE-
TWEEN THE PULITZER BROTHERS, OWNERS
OF THE *Worlds*, AND ROY HOWARD, OF THE
SCRIPPS-HOWARD NEWSPAPER INTERESTS,
PUBLISHERS OF THE *New York Telegram* AND
OTHER PAPERS."

Telephoned Lindsay Parrott and assigned
him to story of *World's* sale, informing him of
Paul Block's withdrawal from transaction, and
asked for flash on decision as soon as ren-
dered. He asked if Friday morning's paper
would be published. Told him I did not know.

Another bulletin from City News:

"BRONX POLICE WERE CONFRONTED WITH
A MURDER MYSTERY TODAY (THUR.) WITH
THE DISCOVERY OF THE BODY OF A YOUNG

WOMAN ON THE EMBANKMENT OF MOSHOLU
AVENUE, WHICH RUNS THROUGH VAN CORT-
LANDT PARK, ABOUT 500 FEET FROM THE
JEROME AVENUE ENTRANCE. THE WOMAN
HAD BEEN STRANGLED ELSEWHERE, APPAR-
ENTLY, AND HER BODY HURLED FROM AN AU-
TOMOBILE TO WHERE IT WAS FOUND. A
LENGTH OF CLOTHES LINE HAD BEEN DRAWN
TIGHTLY THREE TIMES ROUND HER NECK
AND HELD IN PLACE BY A SLIP KNOT."

Looks like good story. Who is she? I called
Lewis at Police Headquarters and Spalding in
Bronx to watch for identification of victim.

Mr. Barrett phoned from Rogers' home. He
still was without rest. Told me he would be in
later and that I should go ahead with things
at the desk.

Began preparation of day schedule. As-
sumed sale of paper, if consummated, would
be story of the day. Put that at top of rough
draft of schedule. Wondered if any story
would break that day which would drive
World story from first position, but thought it
unlikely.

Watched clock as eleven neared. Parrott

phoned that there would be no decision until four. Surely must go ahead with preparation.

City News copy, Standard News copy, newspaper clippings from morning and evening newspapers, poured over the desk. Telephone calls, money orders, visitors, orders on the Morgue, interruptions without end.

"Judge Allen upholds Bank of U. S. indictments." It goes down on schedule with Norton covering, albeit I suspect Allen Norton is sleeping the just sleep that comes to all good morning newspaper reporters until noon.

"Seabury witness at open hearing says it without flowers about Magistrate Jean Norris." It is down on schedule with Hickman Powell covering. Photographer at hearing, assigned overnight.

Members of the staff drift in. "Is the paper to be sold?" "Will jobs be lost?" "Do we publish in the morning?" Who can answer these questions? I wish I could.

No word yet on identity of strangling victim.

Roy Sloane arraigned in West Side Court. Too bad, for his mother's sake, that boy is in trouble again. He must be a bad one, after all.

The city room fills up. Telephones. Three wires on the desk in constant use. The bells ring like an incessant alarm.

Applause rings out in the big room. Clapping of hands and cheers. Jim Barrett is here. I'm glad. Half a dozen try to get his attention at once. No use in my trying to talk to him about mere news. They crowd about him. Every inch of the city-desk platform is taken.

Woodford phones. He is assigned to local politics. Says Macy is out of town, but will try to see Ward.

It is afternoon. Strangely, above the noise about the desk the tingling of the bell on the City News machines denoting imminence of bulletin is heard. A boy dashes through the room to the desk. Bulletin:

Vivian Gordon, 32 years old, 156 East 37th Street, who was to be questioned last Friday by investigators in the Appellate Division's inquiry into magistrates' courts, regarding information she said she had about vice-case frame-ups, was found strangled to death in Van Cortlandt Park today.

So this is the young woman who was found murdered in Van Cortlandt Park. She was killed to keep her mouth shut. Well, this IS

a story. To hell with the sale of the *World*!
This is a real story, the best since the Rosenthal murder in 1912. Charlie Stutz, Hickman
Powell, Sayre Rose, Jack Price, here it is—
the best murder story in nineteen years.

The schedule is changed. Vivian Gordon
murder, with its various ramifications, goes at
the top; the *World*-sale story trail.

Reporters, artists, photographers, editors
milled about Barrett's desk. He shows no sign
of sleepless night. His eyes are bright and his
demeanor snappy. An order of bacon and eggs
lies untouched on his desk; telephone receiver
is ever at his ear.

Kavanaugh's copy from Ossining. Prepare
at Sing Sing for double execution tonight.
We're not so badly off. Think of what these
fellows are facing.

More on Vivian Gordon. She had written
Kresel, asking to tell story of how she was
"framed" in vice scandal. Made appointment
which she never kept. Looks more and more
like Rosenthal case. Look down the long room,
but can see no reporter who worked on Rosenthal story for *World*, nor can I think of any
man at present on the staff who did so. Re-

member that Barrett worked on it for *Morning Telegraph* when he was newly arrived in New York from Colorado.

Barrett remains besieged. He is trying to get down to the news of the day, but the men and the phones won't let him.

The afternoon wears on. As four o'clock nears there is an air of expectancy. Telephone. No decision until seven. Barrett swears pleasantly.

A. P. copy, City News copy, Standard News copy, clippings from afternoon papers, pile up on the desk. So much noise, so much confusion, so much doubt, so much apprehension make it difficult to concentrate on reading of copy.

Finish rough draft of last assignment schedule ever to be prepared for the *World* and pass it over to Jim Barrett. Between telephone calls he glances at it and turns it over to his secretary to put in typewritten form.

Summoned to news conference at 5:20 in Mr. Barrett's absence—the last one ever to be held. Present: R. E. Renaud, managing editor; Herbert Gaston, assistant managing editor; J. Earl Clauson, assistant managing editor; Ben Franklin, night city editor. Mr. Renaud strong for Vivian Gordon murder story. Asks for special story on Rosenthal murder, directing attention to similarity of motive. Says there is little doubt we will publish tonight. Nobody knows as a certainty. Following conference, Ben Franklin takes charge of night city desk with its multifarious worries.

Nothing to do now but go home and await final word. Hear that decision will not come until 9:30 or later. Home to dinner, but too restless to stay there. Back in office. Waiting; still waiting.

Decision comes a few minutes before midnight. The *World*, our *World*, is sold.

Something tugs at the heart and swells in the throat.

Good night.

Over fifty persons awaited the Judge's sentence at the Surrogate's Court—the two who got it to the World *office in three minutes describe how this was done.*

THE DEATH WATCH AT SURROGATE'S COURT

By W. H. Garrison

Watching the South Door

and

Emily Genauer

Watching the East Door

IT WAS our last assignment for the *World*. The setting in the Hall of Records was as packed with drama as if Belasco had staged it. Every newspaper had from two to five men on the story—they had been milling around in nervous groups from 8 P.M., at which time the decision was to have been made—each succeeding hour brought more tension, and the excited whisperings rose in a steady crescendo, until at eleven o'clock every passer-by was besieged with questions.

Talcott Powell, chief of the *Telegram's* forces, strove to bring some order out of chaos by asking everyone present to subscribe to a plan which provided that in the event there were only two copies of the decision, the first would be taken by a City News man, and the second read off to the rest of the men. There were dissenting voices on all sides, and a *World* reporter demanded the right to a copy, as the news concerned his paper more than any other present.

It was then correctly reported that there would be fifteen copies, and an agreement was reached whereby a man designated from each of the news services and all of the morning newspapers, should receive his copy first, the afternoon papers following, then the magazines. This left out more than forty men present.

It was about eleven o'clock now. All the reporters had made plans to rush to the telephones on the ground floor and flash their papers as soon as anything broke. But there were two phones on the fourth floor about which they knew nothing. In one a United Press man was posted, with his partner waiting upstairs in the corridor. In order to keep a line open to his office and to pass the time, he had been joshing with one of the telephone operators for at least an hour. In the other booth was Slobodin, a *World* man. Upstairs we had a copy boy with us. The plan was that as soon as the decisions were handed out we would rush the boy down to the man in the booth with a bulletin to the office, and then we would dash across the street with the ruling itself.

More waiting. Some one opened a window in the corridor because it was getting warm, and from the river we heard the shrill, long-drawn-out siren of a tugboat. It sounded like a banshee's wail, or a dirge. And we reminisced about the old glory that had been the *World's*; of its bright stars, Frank Cobb, Charlie Chapin, Herbert Bayard Swope, Irvin S. Cobb, and the others; of the old *World* dinners and the men who made them history— Alexander Woolcott, whose speech once stopped the dinner, and Donald Henderson Clarke, who also stopped a dinner once because he insisted that some one at the next table was making faces at him; about old J.P.

112

himself, who at that moment must have been turning over in his grave like an electric fan; about his glorious, brave career, and some one even remembered, how, totally blind, he came down to the office once to find out whether the columns in the corridors were round, as he had ordered them, or square, as he had heard. And we speculated—at a New York without the *World*, about what we would do for work and how much profit there was in a box of apples, and if perhaps some *deus ex machina* couldn't still save us.

Time fugued. Some one wanted to know whether Judge Foley was paid on time or space. About eleven-thirty, Williams, of the *Times*, who had been assigned to cover the judge's house all afternoon, came in with Dick Cummins, the chief clerk of the court, and a bulky package under his arm. He had driven down with Cummins in a cab and they had the decisions with them. Much excitement, but could learn nothing. Williams was as much in the dark as we. I went up to the stenographer's office on the sixth floor and stood by as he phoned his desk to tell them he knew

113

nothing yet, but that the stuff would be ready in twenty minutes.

And still more waiting. The excitement was growing greater continually. Several of the men were scurrying about the corridor, making arrangements to phone their offices. The elevator operator had stopped his car on our floor, ready to take the crowd down as soon as we got the decision. Such delirium had never been seen in Surrogate's Court before. In fact, I had always complained that it was dull and nothing ever happened there! Now we were dying in a blaze of glory right on my beat. It was the biggest story we had ever had.

Along about midnight, just when we had become resigned to spending the night in court, we saw Dick Cummins come out of his office. There was a mad scramble. The decisions were finally ready. Powell got out his list, ready to call the roll. But there were only fourteen copies and five times as many reporters, and all vestiges of system vanished in the dizzy rush.

We somehow got a copy. We scanned it, gave a bulletin to the copy boy, and almost threw him down the stairs in our haste to get him to the fourth-floor phone. We dashed into the elevator and, as we darted out of the building, caught fleeting glimpses of an insane free-for-all for the use of the telephones. I don't know how we ever crossed Park Row, but one of us stopped traffic, and the other, armed with the decision, bolted across. Through Perry's drug store I reached the elevator first, and held the car. Straight up to the twelfth floor, where, breathless, we raced into the city room. They already knew that it was all over; that Judge Foley had ruled the sale of the paper permissible.

In accordance with the customary routine, the night City Editor takes over the desk to act as midwife for the last five editions of his paper.

THE LAST NIGHT

By Ben A. Franklin

Night City Editor

CHARLIE CHAPLIN "joined" the staff as a special correspondent on the last night of the *World* and told about his interview with George Bernard Shaw. We should have known it as an omen of tragedy.

A sixty-year-old mother, dumb for four years because of a paralytic stroke, suddenly found her vocal cords loosened by the shock of tragedy she was helpless to avert, and croaked, "My boy!" as her son shot himself to death in an adjoining room.

A woman was found murdered in Van Cortlandt Park.

It was another "murder" that kept men and women of the *World* staff in the office long

116

after official "good nights" from the night city desk. Workers from other departments joined the low-talking groups scattered about the city room. Men wandered in from the *Evening World* office, from the Sunday rooms, from the business office. Reporters gave up their night off to come to the *World* office and be a part of what most of them suspected was to be the death watch.

In that spirit of tension, the night started with Alex Schlosser, assistant city editor, outlining his news assignments of the day to Herbert Gaston, acting night managing editor; Ralph E. Renaud, managing editor; J. Earl Clauson, assistant managing editor, and myself.

We agreed that the murder in the park of Vivian Gordon, who had told the Seabury vice investigators a few days earlier how she had been "framed" by police, was to be the lead story of the paper until Surrogate Foley made known his decision, delayed three times during the day, whether the *World*, *Sunday World* and *Evening World* could be sold to the Scripps-Howard interests.

Charlie Stutz wrote the murder story. About

an hour before the first edition deadline, which was 8:15, he brought his first page of copy to me. His lead, as I remember it now, ran something like this:

"Vivian Gordon, who knew too much about the police framing of women in vice cases, was murdered early yesterday to keep her mouth closed."

I suggested that the lead went further than the facts we had to go on. We talked over a possible lead for several minutes and then Charlie, on the basis of those suggestions wrote a new lead which ran through all five editions. Just before first-edition press time, City News sent out a bulletin that an unidentified man had been taken into custody by police for questioning after they had had opportunity to read the diary of the murdered woman.

To show the world that the *World* still was functioning as a newspaper, though the heavens might fall at any moment, we made the new information a bulletin lead-all and set it in boldface.

Bill Garrison, temporarily doing ship news, was over at the Hall of Records, waiting for the decision. He had been instructed to grab a

118

copy and get it to the office with all speed. Roman Slobodin, our Columbia University correspondent, was sent over with orders to telephone a flash on the decision while Garrison was racing with it to the office. Miss Emily Genauer was also sent over.

Meanwhile, Allen Norton, surrounded by busy talkers, worked away methodically on the last exclusive local story the *World* was to print. Thanks to his efforts during a day which might well have exhausted the spirit of any ordinary reporter, the second edition of the *World* that night revealed that Isidor J. Kresel and four other directors of the closed Bank of United States were to have an early trial. The story also disclosed the assets and liabilities of some of the bank's bankrupt affiliates.

Came 11:15 and still no word from the Hall of Records. Managing Editor Renaud, nervously pacing around the crowded city room, came to my desk.

"How are you going to play the story, Mr. Renaud, provided Foley approves the sale?" I asked.

"We'll have a three-column head on the left [the second most important position on the

119

front page of the *World* and on most news-
papers]. We're going to play the news as news
until the last."

"What!" I exclaimed in horror and with
some choler, I must admit. "Do you mean to
say that the murder of a bum is of more importance or interest to readers of the *World*
than the fact that they will never be able to
read the *World* again?"

"Well," he replied, "that's the way we're
going to play it. We don't know yet if this
will be the last day the *World* is published."

I indulged, I do not regret to say, in pro-
fanity. A few minutes later he emerged from
his office, in which sat Walter Lippmann, editor, and Florence D. White, general manager,
and told me that the *World* story would re-
place the murder story and lead the paper if
Foley permitted the sale.

By this time, it was 11:30. The second edition had gone to press. Slobodin had telephoned from the first floor of the Hall of Records that the photostated copies of the
Surrogate's decision would be ready in ten or
fifteen minutes. He would call again in a few
minutes, he said, and keep the wire open.

Everything was ready for the telephone flash, he reported.

The telephone rang.

"It's the *Daily News*," explained Jack Fahy, in charge of copy boys and phones. "They want to know if we have the decision."

Don Marshall, assistant city editor, picked up the phone. The city desk of the *News*, New York's leading tabloid, wanted to know where Foley's decision was being made public. When Don told them and added it was expected at any minute, the voice on the other end said:

"Gee! I guess we'd better have a man down there!"

To us that was worth a laugh, even if hollow.

Minutes passed. In twos and three and finally in bunches, the *World* staff huddled around the night city desk. The phone rang again. I leaned toward the instrument. It might be the decision; it might be merely a Brooklyn district man reporting a suicide.

"Here's Slobodin." The group around the desk drew closer.

"Hello, Ben. Slobodin again. The clerk is just starting upstairs with the copies. He said something as he passed me about Foley not

121

passing on the contract. We'll know in a minute."

Moments of more tension. It seemed to me and to the hundred grouped around the desk that Cummings, the Surrogate's clerk, must be crawling on his hands and knees to the sixth-floor room where the copies were to be distributed.

Suddenly over the phone I heard feet racing down the stairs in the Hall of Records. The decision was out. Where was that ————— ————— copy boy?

"Here are two United Press men," Slobodin shouted into the telephone, "standing under the only light in the hall. I'll see if they can tell me."

Silence for a moment—then Freddie Jewell, news-machine tender, walked out of the ticker-room, forced his way through the group standing behind me, and laid on my desk:

BULLETIN

NYCNA   B—

SURROGATE FOLEY APPROVES SALE OF
WORLD.
————   11.56 PM

Managing Editor Renaud read it aloud over my shoulder.

Silence. Then, "Here's Garrison!" some one shouted. Out of breath, his face a deep carmine, Garrison flung the fourteen pages of photostat on my desk, and drew his first deep breath in minutes.

I grabbed the last page.

"Submit decree on notice settling the account, construing the will and containing appropriate provisions in accordance with the foregoing conclusions. . . ."

No meat there. I started reading snatches of the decision aloud while Lindesay Parrott, standing by my left arm, jotted down quick notes for a hurry-up third-edition lead.

Page three: "I hold further that there is an implied power of sale in the will, which, in the present crisis, may be exercised by the trustees."

Page by page went over to the copy desk to be read before it was shot upstairs to the composing-room.

"Take that 'e' out of 'developes,' Don."

The group around the desk melted away, Parrott began banging out the end of the *World* furiously at his typewriter. No copy boy could be trusted to carry such precious copy. Instead, Allen Norton and other staff mem-

123

bers bore each paragraph of new lead to me, scanning them rapidly as they made their way to the desk. Behind Parrott stood other reporters watching the copy flow under his fingers. Deadline. New lead ended. Proofs down of the decision. O. K. Send her away. Now for the fourth edition.

Another new lead. More highlights of the decision. An announcement from the Pulitzers expected any minute. Gene Thackrey, go down to 15 Broad Street, offices of Pulitzer attorneys. Brothers down there pouring over decision. See if we can hurry things up.

Nearing the deadline. Roy Howard, new owner of the *World*, the *Evening World*, the *Sunday World*, calls up the business manager. Wants full-page ad of new *World-Telegram*. His statement must go on Page One. Kick out eight columns of news. Going to hold the fourth edition until we get Pulitzer statement. New lead. Insert in new lead. Add new lead.

Finally Pulitzer statement. No more *Worlds*. Make it two-column brevier.

"Trustees of the newspapers to whom Joseph Pulitzer intrusted the duty of carrying on . . . made every possible effort to avoid a

124

sale. . . . For forty-eight years . . . done
its duty. . . . To its army of readers . . .
says good-by. . . . Trustees cannot pretend
it is anything but painful duty."

"Parrott, be sure to get that $500,000 to be
distributed to employees near top of new lead."

Then Howard: "Consolidation means not
death . . . but rebirth." . . . Shoot it
along. Better go up to composing-room to see
the story is put together right. Finally all the
type is in. Let her go!

A fifth edition for corrections.

And don't forget Lena Burlott. Lena, a
hard-eyed damsel and author of a series
printed in the *World* only a month before on
life in the Bedford Reformatory for Women,
her home for more than a year, had been
"kidnapped." The typical threatening note
had been received by Lena's mother. Now
Lena was back home with a lurid tale of having been held prisoner by four men in a hut
near New Haven, Conn. Escaping, she made
her way to New London, which is farther from
New York, and there got a ride home with a
friendly motorist. That was her story and that
was the story the *World* printed. Inconsequen-

tial? Of course, but we had grown to look upon Lena as more or less of an office character. She had been in the office several times. Doggerels had been written about her.

So the *World*, with twelve columns of its own swan song, rolled along to its death.

Mr. Parrott, almost a visitor on the World, *wrote the last copy sent to the composing-room for the final news edition for February 27th. The story told the world that the* World *was no more.*

THE LAST STORY

By Lindesay Parrott

THIS, as I understand it, was to have been the story of a story, some account of the authorship of the three columns of type in which the *World*, early in the morning of February 27, 1931, announced its dissolution.

That story—at least, so far as I know, sent to the composing-room, was published under my name, written, appropriately enough, by a comparative newcomer to the paper—I had been a *World* man just four months.

But, as every newspaperman knows, the writing of all stories is the same. It is, in effect, simply the transposition, with a certain amount of mechanical labor, of a certain number of facts from their original to their typewritten form. And when you have noticed the purely fortuitous circumstance that the last story of the *World*, in its last edition, begins with the word "sale" and ends with the word "consolidation," very little remains to be pointed out with regard to its actual composition.

The story was written in a city room which, as the writer had no chance to observe until later, was crowded as it had never been before. The tension of that crowd of staff men, their visitors, the working press of other papers, ex-*World* reporters and their editors, was, so far as I was immediately concerned, negatived by the tension that goes with work to be accomplished, and accomplished quickly. And the same, I hazard, must have been true of all the others who, at the moment the *World* died, were actually engaged upon the active obsequies—Ben Franklin, the night city editor, who edited the story, whatever copyreader handled it, the linotyper, and the make-up man involved, whose names I do not know.

However, though the story of the story— that is of its actual writing—is therefore an

impossibility, some of the unwritten details
of the gathering of the written facts that made
it may be appropriate. They are here as they
appeared to me, as, elsewhere in this book,
they are recorded as they appeared to others.

First of all, when it at last occurred, the
World's collapse was no surprise. Three days
before, the trustees of the Pulitzer estate had
made their application for its sale to the
Scripps-Howard interests. When, from that organization, no announcement was forthcoming
that the *World* papers were to be continued,
it became evident that they would be, politely,
"merged," or, impolitely, "scrapped," immediately on transfer.

For three days *World* men had worked on
angles of the story—the hearing before Surrogate Foley, the proposals by the Gannett
papers and Paul Block to put in rival bids, and
the (as Roy Howard called it) gallant but
"foredoomed" attempt of the employees to take
the papers over as coöperatives.

So that, in the first edition of the *World*
for February 27th, before the Surrogate's decision came, the story of the negotiations was
not fresh news and ran under a one-column

head, while Vivian Gordon's murder led the paper.

Nevertheless, considerable effort went to the making of the one-column-headlined story.

It was eleven o'clock in the morning, two hours before the usual reporting time, when Alex Schlosser, on the day desk, telephoned to me, at home, that I would write the story for the day. John Gibbs and Philip Pearl had handled it before.

At that hour, the decision was expected momentarily. Surrogate's Court was covered— at an hour few morning newspaper reporters are elsewhere than in bed. There was the probability of what the trade would call "an early break."

That possibility had faded even before I reached the office. The decision was deferred until 2.30—then until 5.30. That, at least, was the word to waiting newspapermen from the only official immediately available—Surrogate Foley's clerk. Court clerks are not necessarily reliable.

"Better go over there. They may slip something over," were the desk's instructions.

Other city editors, all over town, felt the

same way, apparently. In the Hall of Records perhaps fifty men waited, that afternoon, for a surprise decision, until, at half past six, the word came definitely from the surrogate that no opinion would be handed down till late at night. There was F. Raymond Daniell, who wrote the story for the *Times*, Ishbel Ross, who wrote it for the *Herald Tribune.* And during the afternoon and evening more than half the *World's* reporters and at least two editors were, at one time or other, in the courtroom or in the corridors outside.

Elsewhere in this volume you will find the details of that death-watch by the men who kept it until midnight, when the photostats of the decision finally were given, simultaneously, to all the newspapers. My own part became the writing of the story from edition to edition, inside the office.

Two columns was the space allotment, to stand until the surrogate's decision was made public. There were four outstanding features of the story—withdrawal of the Paul Block bid, made in a letter to the Press Publishing Company; an offer from Grank Gannett of $500,000 cash and of a better price (amount not specified) than the Scripps-Howard's; an offer of $5,250,000 from William Griffin, publisher of the *Staten Island Advance*, for all the properties "tangible and intangible" of the three *Worlds*; and the continued fight of the employees. Under this last heading there was the intervention by Gustavus Rogers, attorney for the Employees Coöperative Association in the proceedings before the surrogate, on behalf of the editors promised ten per cent of the *World* stock by the will of Joseph Pulitzer, the elder, to be chronicled. And there was the announcement by J. F. Bresnahan, business manager of the *World* and the *Evening World*, that two Wall Street houses had of their own accord come forward with offers of assistance to the employees' movement.

Again, instructions from the desk:

"Get it all in," said Franklin, "but don't give the employees any better break than anybody else."

Judge for yourself if, up to its last night, the *World* was fairly edited. In the first edition the facts of the employees' moves, that day, are written somewhere in the second column of the story, under an introduction that detailed the long postponement of the ruling from the surrogate and the outside offers for the *World* properties.

Now for the final story; these were the mechanical arrangements:

The surrogate, with his chief clerk attending him, wrote his decision at his home. There John Denson, a one-time copy-reader, turned reporter, waited to telephone the office when the ruling was sent downtown to the courthouse.

Sometime after nine o'clock that news came in. The document was on its way.

In the Hall of Records—in the only lighted courtroom in the building, Foley's—Bill Garrison, a ship-news man *pro tem*, but for the night pressed into work ashore long after hours, waited for it. Like myself, who wrote the story, Garrison, who brought the final news into the office, was a new man on the *World*. We came on the same day.

At ten o'clock, or near that hour, he also telephoned. One copy of the ruling had been sent. The photostats were being made. They would be on hand just before midnight.

Meanwhile, to Ralph E. Renaud, the execu-

133

tive editor, there came a message from the
trustees of the estate, Ralph, Joseph, and Herbert Pulitzer, from their attorneys' office. They
would have a statement to be published when
the decision came. You can read that statement, set two columns wide, on the front page
of the last edition of the *World*. It set aside
$500,000 for the employees, out of the pro-
ceeds of the sale, called that sale "a painful
duty," and said good-by.

That was the line-up when the final news
arrived. It was 11.45. Garrison—he never
wore his hat straight, and that night it was
hanging by a hair—came, almost running,
down the corridor that leads—that led—into
the city room.

He had the photostats. They went directly
to the executive editor's office, were skimmed
through, were transferred to the night desk.

Franklin read them rapidly, tossed them,
page by page—buff-colored photographs of
the original typescript—to the copy desk.
Over his shoulder I had seen enough for a
few paragraphs of "lead," superimposed on
the old story of the first edition.

The surrogate approved the sale, ruled that

he had no power to entertain specific offers for the properties. With that, a new edition of the *World* went to press.

Then the announcement from the Pulitzers; it was the expected.

"The three papers," read the sheet of flimsy sent down from Renaud's office, "will be merged with the *New York Telegram*, under the title *The New York World-Telegram.*

Around my desk as that was written for insertion in the story, under the news of the approval of the sale, there may have been some fifty men, pushing forward for a glance at the trustees' decision.

"This is the last edition of the *World* in its old state," the insertion read.

And those, I think, were the last words read by anyone that night.

The *World* was gone.

One of the World's *most experienced reporters describes the great nerve center of the City Room in the hour of its final agony.*

CITY ROOM

By John J. Leary, Jr.

Industrial Editor

DISCIPLINE, generally speaking, is a loose thing in newspaper offices.

This was particularly true of The New York *World.* Everyone there knew and bowed to authority. But there were few rules. Executives addressed their men as equals and familiars. Men would talk back. Sometimes the arguments would be snappy. Usually, but not always, the executive would have the last word, the work in hand would be done, and that would be the end of it.

Rarely were men discharged. In the last decade of the paper's existence, I recall but two. And in the case of these two, every man on the staff was agreed, to use the vernacular, "they had it coming to them."

The orthodox believer in "rules" would have found the place impossible. There were, so far as I ever knew, no written rules; in fact, but one unwritten rule—one must not "let the paper down." The two men discharged had broken that rule more than once. Blind worshipers of the great god discipline would have fled the office as a place afflicted. Yet when the crash came, when men might well have been excused for panic and sabotage or worse, the one thing that stood out was discipline.

The proceedings that were to end the life of the *World* were made public on Tuesday. My first knowledge of them came as I emerged from the surf in Miami and was handed an Associated Press dispatch. Three hours later I was on my way to New York, and in less than forty in the office. En route, I had read bits of the court proceedings and the fight being made by the city editor, James W. Barrett, backed by members of his staff, to save the papers. I was, therefore, prepared for excitement and, possibly, something akin to a breakdown of the machine.

I found nothing of the sort. Barrett, on

duty somewhat earlier than usual—as a matter of fact, he had not been to bed—was asking what had been done in the case of the unknown young woman, later identified as Vivian Gordon, found murdered in Van Cortlandt Park.

Alex Schlosser, who had been the "right-hand man" of *World* city editors since he had left school, responding in the momentary absence of Thomas B. Hanly, day city editor, said Charles Stutz had been assigned to the case.

"Get the photographers on the job and give Stutz all the help he needs," Mr. Barrett directed. "This will be a good story for days if not weeks."

"I thought they were going to put you out of business today," I remarked, after we had exchanged greetings and he had commented on a souvenir I had brought from Florida.

"I don't know about that," he replied. "Surrogate Foley has promised a ruling this afternoon, but that doesn't mean a thing. Meantime we are going to get out a paper and we're counting on keeping going regardless of what they may think they want to do.

If we can get half a chance we'll keep the papers going."

Already, he told me, more than $500,000 had been pledged, that additional pledges were flowing in, and that "everyone is playing the game."

Mr. Barrett then told of some men whom it had been impossible to reach and asked that I try to see them.

This work kept me out of the office until nearly five o'clock, the hour of the editorial council and also the hour set for Mr. Foley to hand down his decision. The early members of the night staff were on duty and "early copy" was flowing over the desk.

The council was over as I went to the desk to report, in time to hear Mr. Schlosser ask for instructions.

"How about overnight assignment?" he was asking, meaning thereby assignments for work effective early the next day.

"Same as usual," replied Barrett.

"But Foley has promised a decision at five o'clock!" suggested Schlosser.

"To hell with Foley!" replied Barrett. "We are getting out a newspaper."

The only thing to indicate that it was not a normal night in the office was the presence of every member of the staff not required on duty elsewhere, and reporters from other newspapers and press associations. Mostly the *World* men were at their desks, writing the news of the day. Those not so engaged were quietly discussing the situation of the *World* and the chance of the employees securing the property.

These discussions were calm and cold. For that matter, the only signs of nerves throughout the evening were among the visitors. Trying to prevent the destruction of a property and to raise the millions necessary to keep it alive seemingly were not things to be excited about.

The only doubt expressed was how Surrogate Foley would decide and how much of an opportunity to act would be given. Of ability to raise the money or to operate the paper, once it was secured, there was not the slightest doubt expressed. Save for the presence of the men from other papers and the absence of extra telegraph wires cut in all over

140

Sold!

the room, there was nothing to distinguish the office from election night.

Shortly after five o'clock word came that Mr. Foley would be delayed at least an hour, possibly two.

"Who is waiting on Foley?" Mr. Barrett asked of Alex Schlosser.

"Denson," he replied.

"Send Bill Garrison up to help him," said Barrett. "Garrison, you hop that stuff down here the minute you get it. Let Denson phone."

The reason for this shift in arrangements was the approach of edition time. Had Mr. Foley spoken at five o'clock, one man could handle everything easily. With the passage of the hours, minutes counted.

About this time there came what every newspaperman knows as a "grape vine," that is to say, a rumor purporting to give the substance of the court's decision.

"Charley Hand," said this rumor, "has it from Foley and has passed it on to Paul Block that the sale goes."

"Is that true?" a very young representative of a news service demanded of Barrett.

"Ask Charley Hand," he replied, reaching for a telephone.

"Foley won't be ready until eleven," he announced as he hung up the instrument. "There will be five thousand to seven thousand words in his decision."

The first edition, carrying the story to date, had then left the composing-room.

"I wish," Barrett said to me, "that you'd see Herbert Pulitzer in his lawyer's office and get what he may have to say on Foley's decision when he gets it."

I found Mr. Pulitzer and his brothers in a smoke-filled office on the twentieth floor of a Wall Street skyscraper. With them were Roy W. Howard, and his lawyers. Mr. Pulitzer looked even more tired than Barrett, who had been on his feet sixty hours. He was in doubt as to whether there would be a statement. Mr. Foley's decision would be long; it would be late and, possibly, not easy to digest in a moment.

"However," said he, "I wish you would thank Mr. Barrett for me and say that if there is any statement I will issue it from the office."

There was a pause. Then Mr. Pulitzer praised the staff.

"The spirit of the men has been marvelous," he began. "I'm proud of them. But they do not understand the situation. When they see things as we do, as they are, they will see that we could not well do anything else. They're a great crowd. I'm proud of them. We will do what we can to protect them. You may tell Mr. Renaud for me that the first five hundred thousand we get for the papers goes to them. Everyone will get at least two weeks' pay. Those who need more will get more. Make it clear that applies to printers, pressmen—everybody." As to holding up the sale to Mr. Howard and his associates if the court approved a sale, Mr. Pulitzer said this was "impossible." "Under the contract already signed," said he, "the sale becomes effective automatically the moment the court speaks."

Ralph Pulitzer and Joseph Pulitzer, Jr., joined their brother as he was speaking.

"This could not be avoided," said Joseph. His eyes were bloodshot and seemed to indicate recent weeping.

"I wish it could have been," added Ralph.

He, too, looked tired and worn. The brothers seemed less happy than the staff.

It was eleven when I returned to the office. The desk men were busy. So were many reporters. Barrett, between almost interminable calls from the battery on his desk, and questions from reporters from other papers, asked what Mr. Pulitzer had to say and called Ralph E. Renaud, managing editor, from his office, that I might repeat it to him.

Meantime some wag had posted on the bulletin board the announcement that steamship rates to Europe had been cut, first having captioned it timely. The crowd of perhaps 150 got a laugh out of this as they earlier had from an advertisement of a Socialist paper for a reporter that was endorsed "taken."

Mr. Renaud said he had heard earlier of the plan of disposal of the $500,000 and repeated it to H. A. Pollard, once secretary to Joseph Pulitzer the Great, and for many years editor of the *Evening World*, Florence D. White, fifty-two years in the Pulitzer service, and John F. Bresnahan, business manager, who had gathered in his office. They had little comment to make. It was, however, apparent that they were prepared for the worst, for Mr. Pollard and Walter Lippmann, who soon after joined the group, had proofs of the swan-song editorials of their papers.

Next to my desk was that of Charles Stutz, pulled out of bed early in the morning to do the Van Cortlandt Park murder, hammering out a new lead on his story. Benjamin A. Franklin, the night city editor, stopped him with a warning on libel.

"Go slow," he warned. "This stuff is libelous."

It did not seem to be of the slightest importance that long before a libel suit could be filed the *World* would probably be out of business.

Those not engaged in preparing copy continued to discuss the situation. All of the discussion centered on "carrying on" the paper for the paper's sake. No one, so far as I could see, was calculating what suspension would mean to him in the loss of work. For that matter, a check-up later showed that not more than five members of the staff sought employment elsewhere until after the paper was officially dead.

Close to midnight a former member of the staff came into the office with a flask of whisky. On any other night the flask would have been emptied promptly. That night no one wanted a drink, so for an hour it lay on Frank Sullivan's desk. About this time 'Gene Young, the telegraph editor, asked Mr. Renaud about the treatment of a story.

"Let it run," said Renaud as he turned to Byron J. Lewis, night managing editor. "There's plenty of space. I'm putting on two more pages for Foley's stuff."

Mr. Barrett had by this time decided on one more move. He handed two letters to Abe Schechter.

"Go down to John G. Jackson's office," he said, "and give these to Herbert Pulitzer and Roy Howard. I'm asking them to hold up the sale to give us a chance to buy if Foley says the Pulitzer's can sell."

Then in a few minutes things began to buzz. A ring on one of Franklin's three telephones that had been ringing intermittently all night seemed to carry to the crowd a special meaning. Discussions ceased as Messrs. Barrett and Renaud took positions behind Franklin.

"It's Denson," said Franklin, after a moment. Then came a tense moment. The desk paused in its work as Franklin made marks on a pad. "The sale goes," he said as he turned from the transmitter. "Foley says he won't interfere with any contract."

"Damn Foley!" exclaimed a woman near him.

"Amen!" said a man.

"What's the next move?" a reporter from another paper asked Mr. Barrett. "Any injunction?"

"I don't know yet," he replied, and joined Mr. Renaud in advising Lindesay Parrott how to write the story. Mr. Barrett, hard pressed and hurried, had found time to be considerate in making the assignment. Parrott had been on the paper but a few months. He could write "30" for it more easily than one who had put his life into its building.

A few minutes later Garrison dashed into the office with Surrogate Foley's decision. This was taken to Mr. Renaud's room, where George Hall read it to the assembled executives. They listened in silence to the end. Then they

147

agreed with Mr. Pollard, who said, "That set-
tles it."

Sheet by sheet Mr. Foley's ruling was
rushed to the composing-room, followed by
the final statements of the trustees of Joseph
Pulitzer's last will and testament. As fast as
these could be typed they were handed to reporters from other papers and press associations.

As the work went on, the oldest reporter on
the staff in point of service called over three
of the youngest.

"We ought to show Jim Barrett and the
world where he stands with us," he said.
"We'll never have our crowd all together
again."

They agreed. Then Donald Goddard, Phil-
lip Pearl, and Abe Schechter passed around
sheets with this line:

> "For a tangible tribute to a dead-
> game man, a loyal friend, and the
> last of a long line of great city
> editors."

"Not more than fifty cents from anyone,"
Goddard reminded his associates.

"No," said Schechter. "Barrett wouldn't like it."

As they started on their way, all hope that the paper would live the week out vanished.

"Everything suspends this morning," said Mr. Renaud.

Shortly thereafter, Herbert Gaston, night editor, called Charles Sarver into the composing-room. "Good night," he said—the *World's* last good night.

The crowd in the office had begun to thin out by this time. As I started to go, Edward Angley, of the *Herald Tribune*, turned to me.

"God!" he said. "They took it on the chin smiling! There's discipline! By God! they're men!"

They were.

In time of stress, when many things might have been pardoned or condoned, men who in happy times showed small if any evidence of discipline had stood without sign of panic or of nerves, each doing his bit quietly and efficiently. It might be the last copy of the *World*, but so far as they could make it, it would be a worthy copy; so far as fate, in the person of Mr. Foley, would permit, they would carry on.

149

*The staff was embalmed an hour after death
a block away, with its eyes full of tears and its
feet on a brass rail.*

AT DALY'S

By D. A. Davidson

EVERYBODY waited for the fourth edition,
to see how the story looked in the paper.
And when the fourth came up it was like a
rather theatrical person who gets off his death
bed, nails himself erect to the floor, and
grandly announces in his last breath, "I'm
dead, my friends, I'm dead."

In just that way the *World* stood stiff on
its last legs and said very plainly in three-
column italics: Scripps-Howard Buy World.
"I'm dead, my friends, I'm dead." When it
collapsed it was all at once, sheer annihilation,
like the one-horse shay.

"Don't believe everything you read in the
papers," somebody remarked, wryly. But we
believed this. The story had come from a reliable source, as we say, and there wasn't any

chance of its being a typographical error. So
we began to feel funny, and John Gibbs said,
"I feel like an intangible asset." We were all
intangible, disembodied, dispossessed. When
the last page of the last story went up, the
paper and our responsibilities and ourselves
were all put to bed, we felt. There was nothing
more to do. End mark. No overnight assignments, no inserts for the next edition, no need
to be careful about getting into the way of
people who had to make the next deadline.
It was an unrequested emancipation, an unhappy anarchy. It was not just the paper, a
personality, or a person that had died, but
law and order, habits, adjustments, thousands
of little routines. It was this way: The world
had blown up. Somehow you were still breath-
ing in a living interstice in this dead universe,
until the next detonation. So, you thought to
yourself, what the hell? It didn't matter any
more about things like rent, or telephone bills,
or your next job, your family, when you got
home or how sober.

Jim Barrett, on an emotional merry-go-
round for two days, came to an abject halt.
He sagged and his chin flopped sadly to his

chest. There were about thirty people around him on the dais at the end of the room. Suddenly he slapped the desk with his hand, perked up, and began to sing. It was that old posy of the German beer-gardens, *"Du, du liegst mir im herzen. . . ."* He knows how to sing. His rococo baritone used to chase the melody down the alleys of four-part songs in the Colorado State University Glee Club.

Everybody sang with him in a kind of mild, cheerful hysteria. It didn't matter how badly you sang or how much out of tune. It was important only to be carelessly vocal, rapturously clamant. There were bottles with melody to help. Everybody found a paper cup, or two. And the bottles weren't filled with water, because what they were filled with took the wax off the cups and curdled it.

We sang easy, noisy tunes, making up the words with a telepathic unanimity as we went along, never more than three or four words ahead of what we were singing. We sang *"Ach, du Lieber Pulitzer"*—meaning the great and traditionally beloved Joseph—reverently and to the tune of *Augustin*. We sang "J. P.'s Body Lies A-mouldering in the

Grave," also reverently. "And Good Night, Herbert. We're Sorry We Must Go"—irreverently. I don't know what made us so cheerful, except that all wakes have that same uneasy bravado. It is thumbing your beak at death and ruin. Or maybe it was that some of us were really terribly sad and very coy about wearing our hearts on our sleeves. It used to be great stuff to kid the rotarians that way on the old *World*.

At 3 A.M. Barrett was snatched off to the managing editor's office. Heywood Broun and Ruth Hale were there. They had come down from the home of Herbert Bayard Swope, a former editor, where they had listened to the gruesome returns direct from the bedside. Broun used to be a newspaper man himself. While Barrett was out, somebody said, "Let's go to Daly's." That was fitting and inevitable, because Daly's was a customary retreat from trouble and sorrow. You enter through what is artfully designed as the back door—"Don't Enter Here," the ignorant are told—of a store. But nobody ever came out of Daly's loaded up with merchandise unless he went in that way.

A couple of dozen ex-reporters, ex-copy-readers, ex-executives started over at once. Another dozen waited outside Renaud's office, and then went in to rekidnap Barrett. But they talked and talked, Renaud in a strangely defensive tone. It was not his fault, not his fault, he protested. "You know today's my fiftieth birthday," he suddenly observed. "Happy birthday to you."

Barrett looked around impatiently. He was tired of words. "That green hat is mine," he whispered to me, pointing to a far table. Then he ducked out as if for an instant, and the green hat and I followed. And the rest of the dozen of us. On the way over he got to singing again, and we joined in, like penny trouba-dours among the empty skyscrapers. Out of some long-entombed memory he excavated an enchanting ditty called "Religious Tolera-tion," with a snappy thunderous *envoi*. It's too bad we can't print it.

The salesman at Daly's guided us to a rathskeller in the basement. Barrett got an affectionate reception and he was made to sing his song over again. "More, more!" they shouted, delightedly, and it became a kind of

theme song, with everybody hammering out
its heavy lilt. It's too bad we can't print it.
The party became gay.

"Let's go back and get out a real last
paper."

I don't know who said that, but everybody
felt the same way. And in a few minutes the
whole party began to funnel out of the rathskeller, when the mammoth figure of Heywood
Broun suddenly plugged the door, and with
him was Renaud, the spirit of restraint and
common sense. "Never mind about putting
out a paper," Renaud said, authoritatively—
it was the last time he was authoritative. "This
is a party, a wake, and there's plenty to drink.
Come on back." He prevailed, and we slith-
ered back.

In the dark imitation rathskeller a curious
atmosphere prevailed. By tacit decree all rank
was abolished, all castes leveled. It was a
pleasant Bolshevism. Nobody was sir, nobody
was mister, not even the white-haired copy-
reader who adjudicated your copy in times
now past and whom you put in your hierarchy
one peg above the editors. Now Heywood
Broun is easy. But this, for instance, was said

155

to him by a kid reporter who in the days before he met so many interesting people would
have greatly valued a Broun autograph.
"Broun," he said, jauntily, "you look just
like Mack Swain, the guy who was in Charlie
Chaplin's 'Gold Rush.' Why don't you double
for him. You could do all the ballet dancing."
Broun smiled warmly. Everybody smiled
warmly. It was a fantastic brotherhood of the
moment, with all the social restraints canceled.
Liberté, fraternité, égalité.

I felt, in this triumphant congress of the
sans culottes, that one or two habitual executives were uneasy at what some popular Marat
or Danton might do. It was the Jacobins' day
and the aristocrats hid their white hands. This
consisted of becoming "regular fellows." You
could be as fresh as you wanted to. You could
say, "Renaud, I think you're wrong as hell."
Nobody could fire us. We were as fired as
we possibly could be. And the man who gave
you your job and to whom you once went hat
in hand to ask for a raise was no less fired
than you were. And no more fired, either.
There was absolute democracy in that. We
didn't meet by our former rank, by our pres-

ent abilities or future prospects. We met in common fate.

We were now getting happy, and this coroner's inquest might have turned into just a convivial Boy Scout *soirée* out of hours. But Renaud, managing editor, asked for the chair. He asked the *sans culottes*. Then, half bent, he supported himself on the table edge and began to speak, gesturing passionately with his whole body. There was a look of anguish on his face, the first indication of how he felt.

"It's gone," he said. "It's dead . . . and this is a funeral party."

Then we realized again. A vast sorrow, a black despond, swam over us, and a smoldering rage. We felt sold out, delivered, rejected. It was a feeling compounded of the stresses of the past three days, of the recollections of many past years, and—it may be —of the not strictly constitutional beverages.

Something happened then that I never expected to live to see. Jim Barrett, the sardonic cherub, the gagman, the hard-boiled ironist, tottered away from the long table and sat down in an alcove, his head in his arms, his shoulders quaking. When he turned up his head again his glasses looked as though they'd been sprayed with a garden hose. He looked like a spanked boy.

"Until an hour ago," Renaud went on, "I was still the employee of the Pulitzers. But now I'm just one of you, and I want to say that ____ ____ ____"

We now saw the other side of a wake. It was a pathetic caricature of tears, a jag of emotions. Some very strong men wept. And a very level-headed woman reporter, who you wouldn't think had any more tears than granite, began to whimper. She had to go home. None of us raised our eyes. Jim Barrett fell asleep, a mammoth cigar fluttering at the corner of his mouth.

Broun very capaciously took the floor. "Spy, spy!" we called him, shook our fists, hissed and booed with extravagant pretense. Broun smiled, and spoke in that warm pidgin-Southern drawl that he gets from God-knows-where.

"Yes, I guess I'm a spy, a Scripps-Howard spy," he admitted, good-naturedly. "But I was a *World* man, too, and I belong here as much as anybody because we're all ex. I'm

sorry to see the *World* die. Nobody's any more
sorry than I am. But it's just as well that Roy
Howard got it. In the last few years I know
I felt that the *Telegram* was often more courageous and liberal than even the *World*
papers, that it was taking the lead away from
them."

He pitied Surrogate Foley for being surprised that intangible assets—good will and
a name—could be worth millions. Broun
spoke well in the fluent, polished style of his
columns, so well that he made it work twice
and used it for a column a day later.

Renaud approved of Roy Howard. "If the
World had to die, I'm glad it was in the lap
of Roy Howard. Would you rather it had been
Hearst?"

"No," we thundered, righteously.

"Or the *Tribune?*"

We shouted, "Yes!" I don't know exactly
what our logic was, but we shouted, "Yes!"

"Well, I'm not defending Howard because
he's offered me a job. I haven't been tapped
for Skull and Bones. I say that because I believe it."

Broun took the floor again and dreamed

159

out loud about a newspaperman's union. "If there were a union, they wouldn't stand for what's happened. There would be a sympathetic strike. I think that day's going to come."

This looked controversial and not nice. So the conversation was turned into reminiscence. Charlie Sarver, make-up editor, reminisced. Renaud reminisced. Broun reminisced. Bill Haggard, copy editor, got very bold. He knew how sensitive a Lucy Stoner was Broun's wife, Ruth Hale. "Mrs. Broun . . . " he addressed her, in violation of the first Stone commandment. She glinted and doubled her fist. "You call me that again and I'll have to sock you." In token of good feeling, however, she called for a song, "Mlle. from Armentiers." Heywood at her side lovingly rumbled away, leading us through a half-dozen uncouth stanzas. Jim Barrett woke up.

"How is it," a minor Robespierre from the sports department wanted to know, "that a paper with the *World's* circulation and advertising lineage didn't make any money? It certainly should have and it still can." He was asking Renaud. This was a regular Roman holiday of emancipation. He didn't say sir. His tone didn't say sir. He wanted to know. Renaud answered, but not like a white-handed aristocrat. He said: "You're crazy. Lots of papers like that don't. I can name half a dozen."

Robespierre wanted to know more. But these proscriptions are embarrassing, and most of us were hungry. So we went up the narrow stairs, the blinding leading the blind, the lame carrying the lame, and we found that it was daylight, about seven o'clock, and that people who didn't work for the *World* were going to business. We went to Childs to eat. Then we went back to the deserted office, because we didn't have any other place to go.

A former World *man who went to Hollywood tells the inside story of a wake three
thousand miles from a coffin.*

SIC TRANSIT GLORIA MUNDI

By Dudley Nichols

O N THE night of March 12, 1931, sixty
men of varying ages sat around crape-
decked tables in a large rotunda dining-room
out on Wilshire Boulevard in Hollywood. All
smoked clay pipes—Irish-wake pipes—and
passed around bowls of strong tobacco. In the
center of the room, between two eight-foot
funeral candles, reposed final issues of the
World and the *Evening World* in a glass-
topped coffin, and just behind these hallowed
corpses stood a perfect model of the Gold
Dome of No. 63 Park Row.

Perhaps that Dome, with its small flag at
half-mast on the miniature flagpole, served
more than anything else to quicken our imagi-
nations and weld together the threescore men
forgathered for the wake.

For all of them had worked at some time or other under the original of that Dome. The oldest of them, in point of service, was Tom Wilkinson, who went to work under "J. P." back in 1883, before many of us were born; and the youngest was Courtenay Terrett, who had come to Hollywood but a few months earlier, straight from the city room of the *World*. Old Tom leaned on his stick with one hand and used his handkerchief with the other —and for all his emotions, said he hadn't had such a rare time in the last twenty years.

The curious thing was that we should ever have doubted the success of this wake.

For one thing, we had no idea there were so many ex-*World* men on the west coast. When the notion of a wake first came up, talking it over with Terrett and Ik Shuman and Jack Francis, we were able to count twelve or fifteen eligibles. That seemed too few, and the proposal languished for a few days, until finally Jack Francis and myself, both at Fox Studio, sat down and wrote the following invitation, dated Hollywood and under the caption of *"Sic transit gloria mundi"*:

163

Three great New York newspapers lost identities which they had had for periods ranging up to seventy years at 1:30 A.M. Friday, February 27th, when Roy W. Howard, acting for the Scripps-Howard Newspapers, received a bill of sale from Herbert, Ralph and Joseph Pulitzer, officers and trustees of the Press Publishing Company. The morning *World*, *Evening World* and *Sunday World* ceased to exist, and a few hours later the first issue of the New York *World-Telegram*, a six-day evening newspaper under Scripps-Howard ownership, appeared in Park Row.

Many former *World* employees are now on the west coast, and it was felt by a number of them with whom the undersigned have spoken that this journalistic tragedy called for some kind of observance on their part.

When a great man dies, his passing from the human scene is marked by appropriate obsequies. A great liberal institution, such as the *World* was, deserves no less from us who have been associated with it in the past in some capacity.

All writers who have had the honor to work for the *World*, no matter for how short or long a time, will no doubt share this sentiment. In fact, all of them to whom we have spoken agreed that it would be most pleasant and appropriate for ex-*World* employees to forgather for a final wake, sit by the corpse for an affectionate last hour, and hark back to the brighter memories of days under the Golden Dome (these brighter memories will omit Saturdays when the ghost walked and the Dome was not golden).

But although everybody appeared to be in hearty favor of the wake, nobody seemed anxious to undertake management of the affair.

And it is with a sense of duty that the undersigned have arranged with Stark's at 5658 Wilshire Boulevard for an "End of the *World*" wake next Tuesday, March 12th, at 7:15 P.M.

With cigars, ginger ale, White Rock and other prohibition beverages we hope to get by on $5 a head. Your check for that amount will be appreciated with your acceptance of this invitation. Or if you have not time to mail your check, telephone Jack Francis at Hollywood 3000 that you will be on hand, and slip him the fin at Stark's on Tuesday.

It will greatly help if we know beforehand who is coming, so that we may reserve adequate dining-space.

As for beverages, if you wish to preserve the best liberal traditions of the *World* please bring your own. There will be plenty of cracked ice and dilutants.

There is no special scheme of organization behind this dinner. No speech-making unless the spirit moves us when we are in the presence of the hallowed dead. And all we have in the way of a program is Mr. Joseph Johnson's noble agreement to preside as chief mortician. But you'll agree that that is an excellent start.

Finally, please acknowledge this letter to Mr. Francis as soon as possible, for addresses are not all certified and we shall assume lack of response to mean that the invitation has gone astray, and shall be put to the trouble and expense of verifying addresses and telegraphing.

Mr. James W. Barrett, late City Editor of the *World*, has placed in the air mail for the special occasion of our dinner the final and priceless issue of the morning *World*, and this honorable cadaver will grace the table.

On the following day it will be laid to rest in California sod and a suitable headstone erected.

For your information we are inclosing the menu Mr. Stark has promised and a list of invited guests. If you can recall any other bona-fide ex-members of the *World*, please notify us or them—them preferably. Everybody should be welcome, providing he actually was associated with the *World* papers. As former newspapermen it is hardly necessary to say that the occasion is informal.

The broadcast was signed by Jack Francis and myself, and before twenty-four hours had elapsed we began to get the surprise of our lives. Telephone bells began ringing and telegrams poured in. There wasn't a newspaper in Los Angeles that hadn't a former *World* man on it in some capacity. There wasn't a motion-picture studio in Hollywood that hadn't three or four. Old-timers appeared from banks and business offices. The alumni list began to spread over the whole west coast. Down in Tia Juana, Mexico, was Harry Pollok, an official

166

THE WAKE IN HOLLYWOOD

of the Agua Caliente Company, which oper-
ates the racetrack there among other things.
Up in Monterey were Samuel G. Blythe and
Bob Edgren. Living lives of retirement in Pasa-
dena, Hollywood, and elsewhere were old Tom
Wilkinson and a handful of others who dated
back to the 'eighties and 'nineties. Robert
Benchley dropped a plaintive line to us that
he had once run a book column on the *World*
for a whole year but nobody seemed to remember it.

Moreover, there were a few sentimental fol-
lowers, including Harpo Marx, and former
newspapermen who had acted as correspond-
ents for the *World*, who had conceived a lasting admiration and respect for the great newspapers, and these wished to be included in the
gathering.

When the list was finally completed it
named the following:

James F. Archibald, Robert Benchley, Ralph
Block, Sam Blythe, Arthur Brisbane, Bob Burk-
hardt, Roy Chanslor, Donald Henderson Clarke,
Martin Curry, Bob Edgren, Guy Finney, Vick
Forsythe, Ving Fuller, Jack Francis, Oliver H. P.
Garrett, Tom Geraghty, Wm. S. Gill, Will T.
Gentz, Samuel Hoffenstein, E. H. Hansen, Cyril

Hume, Jack Hammond, Geo. Herriman, L. Wallace Hopkins, Joseph Johnson, Julian Johnson, Will Johnstone, Jos. Jackson, Abraham Jacoby, Wm. A. Johnstone, Arthur Kober, Ken Kling, Norman Krasna, Jos. Kelly, Fred Locher, Wm. Slavens McNutt, Geo. McManus, Quinn Martin, James K. McGuinness, Herman Mankiewitz, Edwin Justus Mayer, R. A. Mitchell, Dave Markel, Walter Measday, Dudley Nichols, Jos. Jefferson O'Neill Chas. Owens, Harry Pollok, Arnold Prince, Wells Root, Morrie Ryskind, Will Rogers, Winfield Sheehan, Samuel Spiewack, Ik Shuman, Edward Dean Sullivan, Bob Sills, Samuel Small, Lloyd Sheldon, Louis A. Sarecky, Richard Schayer, Walter Sinclair, Harlan Thompson, Courtenay Terrett, Wm. Tompson, Clark Van Benthuysen, Louis Weitzenkorn, Eugene Walter, Tom Wilkinson, Louis Weadock.

As had been promised, there was no formal program. Joseph Johnson, now a Fox Film executive, presided as chairman, and it was not unnatural that his opening remarks gave a cinematic slant on the passing of the great papers.

The long film [he said] upon which was recorded the life of the *New York World* broke abruptly on February 27, 1931. It had been a notable and honorable picture. The film photographed nearly half a century of American life. It had a good cast. It developed fine action and many stars. Some of them still shine. Others can no longer be seen in the flesh, but their faces and their work are still on the positive.

Tonight, through us who survive it, we shall run the fascinating film of the *New York World.* Or better, we shall turn it backwards—all the way through the years to the day of Joseph Pulitzer.

Some one here, I hope, will describe that powerful and melancholy man; will tell us whence came the fierce fire that blazed in his soul; of why, out of its furnace, there ran red hot the genius that fashioned great newspapers and flung forth the banner of a new journalism.

It is really Joseph Pulitzer we memorialize tonight. It was his spirit that gathered us yesterday and brings us together tonight.

Let us hope that there will again soon come to us a journalist of his courage and independence, and above all, of his passionate sense of justice, which guided him even when he was blind—like Justice herself.

As to the wake! Why not a wake? The body of the departed *World* lies before you; but we still live and must laugh.

After that Mr. Johnson merely looked around the room and called upon whomever his eye lit upon to say his say. A great many of the younger men in that room had come to the *World* long after Mr. Johnson's service under the Dome had ended. Likewise the youngsters were unacquainted with most of the old-timers. But none of the speakers could make an extended address. Each came to the point where he said in effect, "Well boys, you know how I feel" . . . And then sat down.

One of the happiest surprises of the evening was the reading of a telegram from Herbert Bayard Swope, who had been "the *World*" for a great many of the younger men present, men who had been hired and fired by that human hurricane during his years as executive editor. Addressed to the chairman of the *World* dinner, at Stark Café, the eleventh-hour telegram read:

I send heartfelt greetings to my friends with whom I was once on the *World* and to whom I am always bound by great memories. I share with them their spirit of mourning for an institution that all of us loved and none of us thought could die— a death made the more tragic by its being so unnecessary. I join with you in saluting the spirit of the *World*—a spirit that nothing can kill, a spirit that quickens us all and which will be kept aflame by yearly invocations such as this. I salute you men, each of whom had a distinctive share in making the *World* great, and that is a journalistic medal of honor that might have been another story to tell had an offer been accepted from a group which

I organized to buy the papers, but think was blocked by a contract which had been secretly entered into, probably for good reasons, but which seem harsh in the face of a plan that would have kept alive the name of the *World*—and its high traditions.

That's all shoved behind us now, but we have left the privilege of friendship, which I claim from you with pride. My affectionate greeting to all, and my congratulations on the good work you are doing.

George McManus and Bob Edgren telegraphed their regrets and felicitated the idea of the wake, and the following wire was received from Sam Blythe, who at the last moment was unable to get down from Monterey:

When I worked on the *World* from 1899 to 1907 it was the greatest newspaper in America. So it was when a lot of the men who will be at the wake worked on it. Moreover, as the *World* was the only New York newspaper I ever worked on I have no divided allegiances and am an old *World* man exclusively. Therefore, if some old companion under the Gold Dome or some sympathetic fellow who followed in the brilliant company that kept the pace after the staff I was on was gone will act as proxy for me and shed an appropriate tear for and drink an appropriate drink to the memory of the grand old sheet, I shall be grateful. I am sorry I cannot be there, but glad also, for it was a live one when I served it and it is painful to think that it died so nauseating a death.

Winfield Sheehan, vice-president and general manager of Fox Film Corporation, rose from where he was sitting between his old friends, Sam Small and Jack Hammond, and in a simple, heartfelt speech harked back to his old days under the Dome, expressing his regret at the loss of identity of the great newspapers.

"I shall always consider it an honor," he said, "to have worked on the *World*."

John Craig Hammond explained why it was that handkerchiefs were being used so freely at this wake.

"I've seen many of those here," he said, "weep in Perry's for less than the death of a great institution. Two of those present once cried over the death of a fly—in a bottle of rum!"

Others who spoke included Sam Small, Tom Wilkinson, Dick Schayer, Oliver H. P. Garrett, Will B. Johnstone, Louis Weitzenkorn, Ik Shuman, Joseph Jefferson O'Neill, Harry Burke and Clark Van Benthuysen. And among the outsiders, Harpo Marx, who attributed the death of the *World* to the loss of Heywood Broun when Ralph Pulitzer refused to publish Broun's column on the Sacco-Vanzetti affair!

Oliver Garrett and the rest reminisced about their days under the Dome. Joe O'Neill made a touching speech. Louis Weitzenkorn proposed that all those present do their bit toward finding jobs for the *World* employees thrown out of work by suspension of the papers.

All in all, though the death of the papers was attributed to many causes, there was no rancor on the mourners' bench. The writer, who felt that the only possibility of perpetuating the *World* would have been for some strong personality, such as Mr. Swope, to have gained absolute control of publication and policy, said in part:

The *World* died from the same cause that made it so very much alive in happier days. That is to say, it drew its vitality from the fierce life of Joseph Pulitzer. And Joseph Pulitzer is dead these twenty years.

In 1910 he wrote his close friend, Dr. Hosmer, who was attempting his biography:

"I never dreamt," he wrote, "of your even attempting to write a sketch of my life, or anything, in fact, except what you could draw from your own knowledge and observation and experience during the last twenty years—a story of misery and decrepitude, to be sure, but still a story of unceasing work and worry. You are the only man living who can speak from actual knowledge about my connection with the editorial page. That feeble invalidish activity was my only thought. *As Mary Stuart said about her heart being left in France as she sailed for Scotland, my heart was and still is in the editorial page and will be in spirit.*"

That was no idle metaphor. Mr. Pulitzer's heart did beat in the editorial page, and its beating was so powerful, courageous, and independent that it went on running the *World* for twenty years after the blind man's death—like a powerful machine coasting to a stop.

It seems to me that a newspaper more than any other human institution is the embodiment of a great personality.

And in conclusion, the writer added:

While the *World* drew the vigorous spark of life from Joseph Pulitzer, Sr., it drew its blood of life from all of us here and from hundreds of others who in their time have served the papers. Just as in the universe you cannot move an atom without affecting in some infinitesimal way the gigantic forces of the cosmos, so each of us, even though he may have worked for the papers but for a day or a week, in some way has influenced the life and growth—and even decay—of the great dailies.

That thought lends significance to this funeral party tonight.

Finally, in celebrating this wake I think we ought to give praise to those employees who did their best to stave off the end. It was a gallant fight foredoomed to defeat. But certainly Jimmy Barrett, in heading the hastily formed Employees' Coöperative, sustained the traditions of the elder Pulitzer. One could almost say he behaved like a son of Joseph Pulitzer if one had not now grown skeptical of the significance of that word.

Courtenay Terrett's sentiments were as follows:

When I first landed in New York, in the fall of 1921, the first paper to which I applied for a job— any kind of a job, so long as it wasn't in the advertising, mechanical, circulation or business departments—was the *World*. As an extremely youthful newspaperman in the Far West and on the Pacific slope I had conceived an almost religious feeling for the *World*, and even my first sight of the dingy old offices and my first gruff defeat by the doorman did not kill my hopes of working for it.

The *World* was then, we must see now, in its last luxuriant blossoming. Throughout the war it had been "Wilson's mouthpiece," the best-informed, best-informing paper in the country, and it was then maintaining its great reputation by its

Ku-Klux Klan and Veterans' Bureau exposures.
But the *World* wouldn't have me, although I tried
again and again; it was not until 1925, in fact,
that it reversed itself toward me by asking me to
come on as a reporter, and then—still to my regret—I couldn't join its staff.

When, in 1929, I finally came to the *World*, it
was obviously dying. I spent a full year on the
paper, departing only six months before it died,
and I shall always remember the brave fight its
employees made to cure a condition for which they
were in no way to blame. Their fight was all the
braver for the fact that they fought on, even though
they knew it was hopeless. I felt almost a deserter
in leaving before the inevitable happened.

Here are the words of Quinn Martin, motion-picture editor of the late *World*:

The *World* was a great newspaper for those who
read it and for those who wrote it. As its film
reviewer I felt and appreciated its utter independence and courage. Along with others who served
long and comfortably on its staff, I regret it had
to come upon such unhappy days.

In concluding the wake at a very late hour,
there arose the question of the disposition of
those last copies of the *World* and *Evening
World* which reposed in their coffin in our
midst. When Jack Francis and I had first conceived the notion of the gathering, we had de-

cided the following day to bury the "coffin"
in a suitable place. On the Hollywood lot of
the Fox Studio there is a writers' street called
Park Row, and Jack had proposed burying the
papers in the garden of Park Row, marking
the spot with a memorial stone.

Later we put this out of mind and thought
to obtain permission from the Los Angeles authorities to bury the papers in the midst of
the news, of the world's goings on—and what
better place than the center of the city's busiest
street crossing.

But the gods of chance were evidently
against this suggestion, for out of the "End
of the *World*" dinner, just as we were breaking up, came the proposal to form ourselves
into a New York *World* Alumni Association
of the West Coast, to meet each February 27th.
And of course the trophies must be available
for that annual occasion. The upshot of all
this was the formation of a standing committee, with Joseph Johnson as chairman, to sum-
mon us together each February 27th, and
meantime to donate the two papers to the Los
Angeles Public Library, with the stipulation
that we be permitted to remove them one day
each year.

VALEDICTORY[1]

THIS is the last appearance of the *World* as its readers have known it. The ownership has passed from the heirs of Joseph Pulitzer to the publishers of the Scripps-Howard chain of newspapers. With this sale the responsibilities of the present editorial direction come to an end.

On page 1 of this issue the trustees of the newspaper properties are making the public announcement of the action they have taken. On this page it remains only for us to say a grateful farewell to the readers of the *World*, to pay tribute to the long line of distinguished newspapermen who over a period of nearly half a century made the *World* what it has been, and to salute those who now become the owners and directors of the newspaper.

We have striven, subject to the limitations of our own abilities and of ordinary human frailty, to carry out the solemn injunction of

[1] Copyright, Press Publishing Company, *New York World*.

178

the founder that the *World* should be conducted "as a public institution, from motives
higher than mere gain," and at all times "in
a spirit of independence." We believe that the
readers of the *World* have shown their faith
in the genuineness of this purpose by the
loyalty with which they have supported the
paper. For such support by its readers the
World is deeply grateful.

To the newspapermen who have worked for
the *World* we pay affectionate homage. They
include many men who will long be remembered in the history of the newspaper craft.
They include an even larger number of those
who, working in the proud anonymity of a
great institution, have given their devotion
and all their strength to its service. The obli-
gation to them does not end this morning.

To the new owners of the newspaper, the
Scripps-Howard organization, and to the editors and staff of the *Telegram* we offer our
best wishes for the future. They are seasoned
newspapermen. They are public-spirited, in-
trepid, and generous. They are competent,
enterprising, and successful. May good fortune attend them.

Farewell! Let the last words of the *World* be those of Mr. Valiant-for-Truth in *The Pilgrim's Progress*:

> "Though with great difficulty I am got thither, yet now I do not repent me of all the trouble I had been at to arrive where I am. My sword I give to him that shall succeed me in my pilgrimage, and my courage and skill to him that can get it."

Walter Lippmann

The World's *dramatic critic was assigned to review the drama of its last hours. He was elsewhere at the time, but that never hampers a really good critic.*

CURTAIN

By Robert Littell

I VAGUELY remember having once seen a play in which a man with a rope around his neck stood up and cried, "You can't kill me!" I forget whether the playwright killed him or not.

Such things happen outside of plays. They happen to men and they happen to newspapers. Like men, newspapers sometimes stand up in a great crowd and shout: "You can't kill me. I am not merely a few dozen sheets of wood pulp dotted with ink. I am alive, I have a face—you can't kill me." And then suddenly they are dead.

The death of the *World* was like the death of a man. Properties are sold, and pass from existence to non-existence without a murmur.

Men die, but in their last agony, in the few days between sentence and execution, between noose and nothingness, they can utter a final triumphant desperate word which will never be forgotten by those who hear it.

The *World*, with the fatal noose about its neck, kept the executioner at bay long enough to tell everyone that it had the will and the right to live. And then suddenly the noose tightened and it was dead.

When people die, for a long while one doesn't believe that they are dead. It isn't possible, it can't be, it is all a mistake, a hideous dream from which we shall wake up. . . . One goes about with a dull, recurring ache; in imagination one lives through those heart-breaking days; one dreams of the things that might have happened to prevent it; one remembers the moments when one felt that perhaps it would all come out right after all— and then one wakes up, at the sight of a news-stand, at a glimpse of some advertisement for the morning *World* still on an elevated plat-form, and realizes, all over again, that the *World* is dead and that nothing will bring it back.

We all felt the noose around our own personal necks during those three dark days, but that was a comparatively unimportant feeling, for the *World*—and some of us were aware of it then for the first time—was far more than the sum of all of us and of all our necks. It wasn't the printed paper itself, nor what was in it, nor what was back of it, nor the great living impulse that still beat through it so many years after the death of its founder—there was something more, something on two legs, with a face and a heart and a helpless, furious desire to go on living. Something so real, and so much more real for being intangible, that I fully expect, on some moonless night, to meet its ghost, the ghost of the *World*, moving with noiseless feet along the pavement of Park Row.

And with that ghost I shall exchange memories of the Tuesday, the Wednesday, Thursday, and Friday that followed Washington's Birthday in the year 1931. By the time I meet the ghost—for I do not expect to meet him until all New York's papers have been merged into one—we shall perhaps be able to talk of how it all happened without bitterness. We

shall remember the city room, grinding out
the next to the last paper as if nothing had
happened, as if everything were to go on happening as usual. And the long hours in somebody's office, waiting, waiting for news from
the lethal chamber, for the latest postponement of Surrogate Foley, while our hearts were
numb and our mouths pretended to the cheerful and wisecracked about the Foley Bergères
or the Foleys of 1931. And how we looked out,
at a New York that seemed heartlessly occupied with its own affairs, through unwashed
windows, and wondered when those windows
would ever be washed again. And how some of
us took refuge in an unfamiliar room where
presided a gigantic bust of Joseph Pulitzer,
and how we tried to get a statement from the
great bronze mask, and how it refused to be
quoted, and what burning words we put into
its inscrutable metal lips. . . .

Disaster does strange things to the passage
of time. The clock ticks unsteadily, and the
hours are telescoped into a stretch of agony.
I cannot remember those last days as separate
days. The story of their ups and downs has

been told elsewhere by the men who were gallantly fighting for a reprieve. In my recollection those days are a lump of tangled hope, fury, and despair. To the weather man they were blissfully mild, a gap in winter so full of sun and blue air as to be almost spring. I don't remember much about the sun or the color of the sky. I remember waiting, waiting, and then feverishly sucking up the latest rumor, and then waiting and waiting again. The curtain on this newspaper seemed to fall, and then was raised a few feet to show us desperate figures pushing their way toward the scaffold, and then it fell again. It kept rising and falling. The noose tightened, and was frantically unloosed, and tightened again. Though one longed beyond all things for the spark of life to keep aglow, at times one also longed to have the poor animal put out of its pain.

I was not in at the death. I was reviewing a show—some dreary little mess of a play that made the real drama that was going on seem all the more relentlessly tragic. A play, as nearly as I could make out, about a young man

who had inherited millions and who, for a
whim, made a princess out of his serving-maid.
A Cinderella temporarily hung with jewels. It
was hard to keep my mind on the play. But it
was equally hard, when my mind was on it,
not to see a connection between every one of
its dreadful features and the tragedy that was
going on at Park Row. The princess of the
play kept turning into a newspaper, and her
end was, not jewels, but ashes. And when some
one in the play wanted some one else boiled in
oil, I found a terrible correspondence with my
own feelings. Between the acts I would telephone down to Beekman 3-4000 and get the
latest bulletin from the bedside of the dying
princess-among-newspapers.

And by the time I had recorded (in that
World uptown office so full of folders of trips
to Havana, Florida, Mexico, and other hints
to the unemployed) the story of the serving-
maid and her rich young employer, the surrogate had finished weaving his 7,000-word
noose.

Curtain

A music critic's confession is the pathetic story of its first assignment which frightened him so much that he had to cry.

A FIRST ASSIGNMENT

By Samuel Chotzinoff

I HAD just sent down some copy about the Philharmonic Orchestra and a promising conductor, Arturo Toscanini, when the word came that in a few hours the *World* would be dead. Had I known that death was so imminent I would have done better with my half a column than waste it on music. There were so many important things for the dying paper to whisper to its friends and relations, things that should outlive the scandals and the flurries of that day. With its last full breath it should have spoken of its noble and merry life, the ideals it followed (ideals exist, and the *World* had a few), the civilized spirit that animated the people who worked for it and the natural sorrow of all the bereaved. But, except for one touching editorial farewell, the

World went down like an Anglo-Saxon ship, the band playing and the radio-operator receiving news to the last.

Had I realized the extreme gravity of that hour I would have ignored the Philharmonic Society and in its place have left a record of my association with the *World*. I would have done this not out of vanity, but because such a story would better reveal the character and the personality of the paper than any impersonal enumeration of its qualities. One of these qualities struck me, I remember, with the fullest force when I walked into Herbert Swope's office one September day in 1925. Deems Taylor had just left the *World* to devote his time to the writing of operas. Deems had been one of the brightest of the literary ornaments Mr. Swope had assembled for the now famous page opposite editorial, and his discarded shoes promised to be as difficult to fill as Cinderella's slipper. The truth was that they could only be filled by Deems Taylor himself. But many an editor would have made the mistake of trying to make them fit some one else.

What Swope knew about me was that I was

a musician and that I had contributed several articles on music to *Vanity Fair*. With such meager qualifications for so important a post I can only wonder now how I summoned the necessary nerve to ask for the job. Much to my surprise, Swope did not instantly have me thrown out of his office. Instead of that he shouted at me that he greatly admired my courage, and began a long and exhaustive declamation about the merits of Mr. Taylor, the main current of which he often sidetracked with anecdotes about the profession of musical criticism. There were a thousand interruptions —the telephone, heads of departments, reporters, and what not. But Swope always resumed his harangue at the exact place he had left off.

"I'll give you a try-out," he finally said. "But if you fail, don't feel badly about it. You may be the greatest musician in the world and yet be quite unable to write an interesting, concise criticism in an hour or an hour and a half. You may be just the right person for a weekly or a monthly magazine, and fall down completely on a daily job. If you make it, well and good, but your failure will be no

reflection on your knowledge or ability, any
more than a man's baldness is a reflection on
his character." He dismissed me. But as I
closed the door behind me he shouted, "And
for God's sake don't try to write like Deems
—or anyone else."

At my next interview with him the executive editor of the *World* outlined my duties.
"You will inform the reader what has taken
place and where. If you like a performer or
a composition, tell why. If you don't like him
or it, also tell why. One thing you must always remember—the *World* has no ax to
grind, and never can have. If my aunt, cousin,
daughter or grandmother should happen to
be the person you are reviewing, you must
ignore the relationship. Another thing, the
World has no sacred cows. Write what you
believe, avoid libel, and you will be doing
your whole duty by the paper. And now let
me show you around."

I was led into the city room, the Sunday-
editorial room and the little cubbyhole that
housed the dramatic, the movie, and the music
departments. F. P. A. was the only man on
the floor who had a room to himself, and I

caught a glimpse of that lanky sage at his typewriter, serenely oblivious of what I then thought was a vast disorder around him. In those days F. P. A.'s door generally stood half open. The partitions of his little room did not join the ceiling and he was constantly subjected to visits from his colleagues and to the intellectual (?) noises that floated in from the dramatic-movie-music department. But his rebellion was not slow in manifesting itself, and presently carpenters had made his den air tight and the always shut door bore the printed warning:

> This is not the office of
> Alexander Woollcott
> Quinn Martin
> Laurence Stallings
> Samuel Chotzinoff
> Allison Smith
> Herbert Swope
> Louis Weitzenkorn and
> Mrs. Ober

Mrs. Ober was the society editor.

Everyone was charming and sympathetic. The place in its disorder and untidiness was the realization of what I had hoped it would be, and I was blissfully happy until the day

of my first assignment. This was a performance of "La Tosca" by the San Carlo Opera
Company, at the old Century Theatre. All
that day I tried to compose an opening paragraph for my review, but I found, to my consternation, that I had forgotten whatever I
had known about syntax, grammar, and spell-
ing. At night I arrived at the theater in a
daze, and found Allison Smith of the dramatic
department in the lobby. Miss Smith informed
me that Herbert Swope had delegated her to
attend me and be of what service she could.

I blessed Mr. Swope and clung to Miss
Smith for dear life. I witnessed the performance through a haze. Presently I was in the
Subway, with Miss Smith at my side, and soon
after in the dramatic-movie-music room in the
World Building. The clock in F. P. A.'s office
said half past ten. Miss Smith stuck a sheet
of paper in a typewriter, told me everything
would be all right and went away. I stared
at the typewriter for a minute and glanced
up at F. P. A.'s clock. It now said eleven. I
sat down again and stared some more at the
empty paper. Suddenly I felt a hand on my
shoulder and I heard the softest, gentlest

voice in the world say: "Have you any copy
for me? I am Joe Canavan, the night city
editor. I don't want to hurry you; there is
plenty of time."

I turned and saw before me a big man with
a big baby face, the eyes covered by a green
shade. I pointed to the inkless sheet and began to cry. Joe Canavan put his arms around
me and said: "That's all right. It happens to
everybody at a first assignment. Now try to
write something. You'll be surprised how well
it will look in print. Just write anything at
all."

He smiled and left me. He came back in
a quarter of an hour, saw that I had typed
a few sentences, read them over, and assured
me that I was doing beautifully and that I
still had plenty of time. I had no idea what
I had written by the time the clock pointed
to one, but Joe told me it was a good piece
and took me with him into the city room and
introduced me to some of the men. Soon he
handed me a proof. "Doesn't it look pretty?"
he said. "I told you it would be all right."

I suppose the attitude of the *World* toward
the problems of local government and world

polity was the height of liberalism and all
that. But I think the attitude of Joe Canavan,
Allison Smith, and Herbert Swope to a be-
fuddled, desperate, would-be newspaperman
like myself was a not less important mani-
festation of the spirit of the great, dead,
morning *World*.

It takes more than a columnist:—a double columnist like Sullivan to tell how he moved in and out of the World.

THOUGHTS BEFORE
THE UNDERTAKER CAME

By Frank Sullivan

ON A day at the end of last February I finished my farewell piece for the *World* and then began the task of clearing out the desk I had occupied for eight and a half years.

It took a major crisis such as had occurred to get that desk tidied up. Many times during my first four years on the staff, when I was younger and had more energy, I had been impelled by attacks of orderliness (vestigial remnants, I suppose, of my old Puritan ancestry) to tackle that desk. But the desk always won. Four and a half years ago I gave up and decided to let well enough alone. Thereafter I stuck all my mail into the top drawer and thought no more of it. The early Pleistocene layers of letters probably sank to the bottom

195

of the desk and became carbonized, like little bugs and flowers that become imbedded in a bog and stay there a million years too long.

How did I get such a desk cleaned out before the undertaker's men took charge of the city room? I cut the Gordian knot by throwing away most of the contents of the desk, probably including my soldier bonus certificate, which I can't find and which I may need one of these days. Some of the contents I saved, haphazard. The aspirin, for instance. Many a day following a rough night, when I approached the desk with one eye shut (the better to see you with, little typewriter) that aspirin was a boon.

Pasted about the desk, behind and beside the typewriter, were the December leaves of eight calendars from 1923 on. They were adorned in varying degrees, according to their years, with the grime and dust of time. Also there was a practically new calendar for the year 1931, only one leaf gone. Annually, at New-Years time, I had pasted a calendar in my desk for ready reference, for, true to the time-honored tradition of all newspaper offices, the calendars in the *World* were hung behind files or in spots where to consult them necessitated standing on one's head and spraining one's neck. If the day comes when I work in a city room where there are plenty of great big calendars, all visible to the naked eye of the reporter, and where the dictionary is not more than forty paces from your desk, and where the page of the telephone book containing the number you want, is not torn out, I may be greatly disappointed. Half the spice of the game would be gone were these little tribulations absent.

The housecleaning finished, I detached the key of the desk from my ring and left it in the desk. I disliked that key; it was always getting lost. At least I won't have to deal with that any more. And there won't be that window behind my desk which Jack Leary always wanted shut and everybody else wanted open. And there won't be the sun which along about May reached the point in the heavens where it began to stream in on my desk, getting in my eyes and retarding or stimulating the hatching of matchless prose, according to my mood of the moment. There won't be the telephone calls when I'm in the middle of a piece.

197

And there won't be the visitors, seating themselves on my desk as I brooded over an idea (just found, after much travail) to tell me jokes that would make the 156-year-old Turk look like a tot.

There won't be any of the minor crosses that used to make me growl. And I'm just beginning to realize how I shall miss them.

I regret now that I left the typewriter (property of the *World*) in the desk. Certainly I should have borne off some souvenir of those eight and a half years, and we had grown fond of each other, that machine and I. Its predecessor was a doddering mass of clattering incompetence that served me during my first six years on the *World* and wrecked what had been a superb nervous system. Periodically I would demand a new typewriter, and not get one. Then one day I said to Jim Barrett through force of habit: "Jim, how about a new typewriter? This piece of junk is falling apart."

The next day a shining new typewriter was in my desk, I went home with a high fever, suffering from shock, and took to my bed for three days.

I recall the evening in mid-October of 1922 when I walked across the cool dusk of City Hall Park from the *Evening Sun* office to the *World* and was hired by Swope—Herbert Bayard Swope to you. I had in mind a gracious address to deliver to Mr. Swope. I would indicate deftly that he was to congratulate himself on securing the services of such a promising young journalist. There was, I believe, to have been a careless reference to an advance in salary.

Swope was dictating to Helen Millar, firing instructions at Bill Beazell and Earl Clauson and talking over the Albany telephone line with Governor Al. Smith—all at one and the same time. My speech was not delivered as planned. It was not delivered at all. H.B.S., however, gave me a trenchant address on the ethics of journalism in general, the place of the *World* in particular, my own good fortune in being tapped for that paper, the influence of Stanton in Lincoln's Cabinet, the best method for making raised biscuits, the Tacna-Arica dispute, and the Schick test for scarlet fever.

I went to work and immediately lapsed into

obscurity. For a month I did something like paste up bankruptcy reports. I suffered the most awful pangs of homesickness for the old *Evening Sun* office.

Then, quite involuntarily, I leaped into what it would be gross understatement to call prominence. A highly respected lady had died. She bore a surname identical with the surname of a prominent young matron, daughter of a famous financier and inheritor from him of a large fortune. Through some diabolical slip of the mind (to charitably paraphrase what really was sheer incompetence on my part) I got the idea fixed in my head that it was the daughter of the financier who had died. She therefore had the rare experience, the next day, of seeing the news of her passing blazoned on the first page of our first edition (it was yanked out of later editions, after a bewildered butler had telephoned our office for details). I paid glowing tribute to her worth. I was highly complimentary to her. There was nothing she could have taken exception to in that obit— except the statement that she was dead. I was told later that after the first shock she was inclined to regard the incident humorously, but it was no joke to me, nor to the editors of the *World*. The fact that they didn't fire me immediately is testimony of the kind of place the *World* was.

Once afterward I met that matron. We chatted for a moment and then went our ways. She never knew that the obviously nervous young man who had blushed furiously on being introduced to her was he who had tried to shove her prematurely across the Styx.

After that incident Jim Barrett confined my activities largely to such trivia as attending demonstrations of kiss-proof lip-sticks and so on. It was all right with me and a period of easy-going assignments followed, out of which I was rudely jolted in May, 1925, by the following note from Mr. Swope:

Adams is going away for more than a month and the brilliant idea has occurred to me to turn his column over to you to play with. You can write long pieces, short pieces, grave or gay. . . . We will hit upon a happy head.

Talk to me about this.—H. B. S.

The only funny part of that clarion call was the last line.

Thus ended the glamorous period of ease, with nights of innocent merriment at the now defunct Roymont Club on William Street, back of the *World*. Thereafter, I was a "feature" on the paper, God help me. I had a by-line. A by-line, I can state from experience, is a device which enables your friends to rush up to you the day after a piece has appeared and tell you how terrible it was.

On a sizzling day in that summer of 1925 I was steaming morosely in F. P. A.'s cubbyhole (while he was traipsing gayly about Europe on his honeymoon), trying to think of something to feed to the vast maw of that broad-measure column the next day. Suddenly I found myself writing a piece about an imaginary new stenographer, Miss Martha Hepplethwaite, who would do no work but insisted on swinging from the chandelier, jeering at me. I was surprised when people seemed to like her. I don't want to seem ungracious, but I never thought Martha was much of a character.

My love goes out to her, however, at this time; and to her colleagues, Aunt Sarah Gallup, the grand old lady of the Adirondacks, and Joseph Twiggle, dean of New York street-cleaners. They were a willing trio and helped me out on many a dull day.

Mr. Twiggle came into being as a result of the flood of ticker tape attending the Lindbergh homecoming. Aunt Sarah Gallup had a more hectic start. I was doing "sidelights" on the Democratic convention in Madison Square Garden in 1924 and had to fill one column a day. One night I found myself a paragraph short. Being in my historic hurry to get goodnight from Joe Canavan, I simply added a paragraph about a fictitious old lady named Aunt Sarah Gallup, from Holcomb Landing near Ticonderoga, N. Y., who had saved her butter and egg money to come to the convention and root for Al. Smith. To give the item piquancy I added that she was 104 years old.

I then walked innocently out of the office and buried my fevered countenance in a tall Scotch highball. Next afternoon at the Waldorf I met Fred Edwards of the *Tribune*. He and I were working together in the accumulation of the sidelights. Freddie was bitter.

"What do you mean holding out on me?" he demanded.

"What do you mean 'holding out'?" I asked. I had forgotten about Aunt Sarah.

"My office asked me why I didn't get that human-interest story about the old lady from the Adirondacks."

I explained.

On reaching my own office I found that poor Alex Schlosser had devoted some minutes of a hot and busy day to locating our correspondent at Ticonderoga, to instruct him to be sure and get a picture of the old lady of 104. The correspondent at Ticonderoga (which is a *bona fide* place, of course) must have had a baffling time trying to locate Holcomb Landing. There is no such place.

I also learned that the venerable Associated Press had been trying to locate Sarah. It was an outrageous hoax, but it was done without malice. I just wanted to get that column filled.

Aunt Sarah stayed. I increased her age to 287 years. That broadened her scope, I thought.

I can't kick. I had eight and a half pleasant years on the *World*. I realize now what an Eden it was. Nobody, from Ralph Pulitzer, the publisher, to Joe Wilcinski, the head copy

boy, ever was anything but friendly and helpful. Nobody bothered me. Nobody told me
what to write or what not to write. When
Swope hired me he told me the *World* had no
"sacred cows." I found that to be true. The
editors were glad when I did a good piece, and
patiently uncomplaining during the lengthy
stretches of the dull ones.

When I die I want to go wherever the
World has gone, and work on it again.

The reporter who became secretary of the employees' association in their attempts to buy the World *explains why he worked perennially without a raise.*

THE *WORLD* PASSES*

By Philip Pearl

FIVE years ago or twenty-five or forty, we started on our first newspaper jobs. We broke in on sheets in Atlanta or Denver or Brooklyn. It was fun and it was achingly dull. We stumbled through our first big story; waited, empty, for the edition to come up, and then saw our first by-line. We hurried out, hugging the paper under our arm, to be alone in a one-arm lunch room. And on the way we bought the *World.*

Perhaps it was only one story that warmed us, perhaps a single phrase that said what we had always wanted to say. We might be thousands of miles away. But it was our paper. In it we saw our size. It held out its arms to us.

* Copyright by *Saturday Review of Literature.*

We hoped for the day when we might be worthy to grow within their embrace.

When the day came we were older. The gilt dome of the Pulitzer Building had taken on a greenish tinge. The pressure of dollars and cents had sapped the spring from our enthusiasms. But in a day, in a week, we found a new, rich, intangible soil to take root in. The rush of wind in the wake of Herbert Bayard Swope. The sudden smile on the cherubic face of Jim Barrett. The nonchalant sureness of Ben Franklin smoking a cigarette or doctoring our copy. Our own lunacies and the tolerant forgiveness. Such things held us to the *World* while we grumbled about inadequate pay, the failings of copy-readers and editors, the annoying exigencies of the immediate job; these and the illusion that we could say the ineffable, achieve the impossible, and that this newspaper could.

Now the *World* is dead. To any newspaperman those five words round out a complete obituary. They tell the story. Newspapermen pretend to despise sob stories. Let us keep up the pretense. Let us say the *World* was only another newspaper. Now it is missing from the newsstands. Let us say it was just a business that tried to earn dividends. Now it has given up the struggle. Let us recite the catechism of reality over and over again, rivet it with desperate reiteration into the brain.

Before the final editions of the *World* are buried in the dust of library files, the time comes for autopsy. It is going to be a very public affair. For years all of us, solicitous or envious, have been trying to diagnose the ills of the *World*. Now each knows why it died. I can find no relief in such post-mortem recapitulations. Here I wish to offer only an appreciation.

The *World* was read in Harlem, in Hell's Kitchen, in the colleges, on the East Side, in Greenwich Village, and, especially, in all newspaper offices. It appealed alike to the intelligent and the simple because it was imbued with a fundamental sympathy. It had a heart. It had courage. It was interested in events chiefly as they affected human beings. At times it grew maudlin over life's little tragedies or great joys. But it could never treat them matter-of-factly.

The *World* did not attempt to print all the

news. For this it was branded as something less than a newspaper. Of course, it always gloried in being a good deal more than a newspaper. But, save in breathless spurts, it couldn't approach the completeness, the mechanical precision, and the impersonal proficiency of the *Times*. It lacked method and organization and direction. It was impelled by motives. Sound or silly, they colored the news. It was starved for space. Editors and reporters alike were disciplined by the physical necessity for selection and condensation. Out of daily chaos there evolved a live, readable newspaper, usually well-written and well-balanced, but quite unsuited as a rule for reference files.

Every reporter, sooner or later, had the opportunity of writing a "Madame Bovary" in half a column or a one-act "Hamlet."

"Good story," he was told by whoever happened to be his boss. "Go ahead and write it."

He scrambled life and literature in a frying-pan and did his best to cook that "Good story." Frequently he succeeded. And we were all proud of him and proud of the paper. And the next day, probably just to keep him sub-

dued, he would be sent to cover a convention
of life insurance presidents. And instead he
would go to the movies or join a bridge game
in the cozy cellar of the City Hall. These were
the heights and the depths.

We tried to write lucidly and simply. We
tried to say what happened and make the story
trenchant and forceful. We also tried, as un-
obtrusively as we knew how, to give the reader
our eyes, to make him see people and events
as we saw them. Such editorializing in the news
was a sin. But we were shriven if we could sin
honestly and expertly enough. If we couldn't,
we went out and got drunk.

Nothing much was said in the office about
traditions. They were to us something like the
words of the "Star-spangled Banner." But the
fighting music always sounded clear, never
more so than in the last year of the *World*.
Here is a story very few people outside the
newspaper fraternity know about.

In its final year the *World* reared up on its
hind legs and fought. In this period it "broke"
more exclusives than all other newspapers in
the city combined. It printed the first story of
the disappearance of Supreme Court Justice

Joseph Force Crater. The other sheets woke up to this news the next morning and were forced to "pick it up" from our late editions. So it was with the whole recent tide of graft exposures. In each case the *World*, if not the only newspaper to investigate, was regularly the first to print the facts.

It was a grand fight. It failed to save the *World*, but it did put new life into its competitors. It startled them out of a long siesta. Greatest achievement of all, it drove reporters to work. It kept them awake night and day. We, too, went without sleep. But it was our show. The others were haggard. They joined forces to protect themselves against the *World* and still they dreaded the next "beat." It couldn't last. They had to catch up with us and they did. Our last stand was over and we had nothing but a libel suit or two to show for it.

Then came months of awful dullness and then rumor. The *World* was to be sold. The tip came to us from lawyers, from business men, from outside reporters. No attention was paid to it. The idea was incredible. It was one

of the few tips the staff of the *World* never
thought worth investigation.

Even when rumor became a matter of court
record it bore no real significance. Perhaps we
were dazed that first day. The second day we
lost ourselves in blind resistance. It was not
until the third day that we sensed the end.

We were reporters. We had seen other people's tragedy. On the last night of the *World*
those of us gathered in the city room watched
and waited for our own. We waited seven
hours from five o'clock until midnight. Some
of us hoped.

Then came back flooding impressions. Of
familiar faces suddenly grown beautiful. Of
brave, frightened laughter. Of a great, com-
munal warmth.

We heard the story of an *Evening World*
veteran. Some months before he had written
his own obituary for the files. By some mis-
chance it got into the paper. He phoned the
next morning to say the story was somewhat
premature. He died the day the sale of the
World was submitted to the Surrogate's Court.

And while we waited for the decision of the
court that night we watched Jim Barrett. He

had forgotten all about his job as city editor. Others were carrying on for him. To him the end of the *World* was no story. It was a matter of life and death and upon him fell the dual responsibility of mother and physician.

There were false alarms. And then, at midnight, the flying figure of Bill Garrison, a photostatic copy of the decision in his hand. We piled, fifty of us, around the desk of Ben Franklin. He remained the night city editor, methodically "slugging" and numbering each sheet before passing it on to the copy-reader. A few minutes later he was fighting, as he had fought so many times before for other stories, to assure the end of the *World* the "lead" position in place of the Bronx murder.

We knew then we were through. We saw it in the awed and sympathetic faces of the visiting, working press. Howard Cushman stole away to his typewriter to write:

"It is not the loss of a job; it is the loss of an ideal, a star, a goal to shoot at. It is as if a young devotee had taken his orders and begun his ministry and then discovered that his God had feet of clay and had sold out to the nearest tabernacle."

The renowned columnar critic, Heywood Broun, was among those waiting at H. B. Swope's house on Friday night for the executioner's axe to fall.

IT SEEMED TO ME

By Heywood Broun

I SAT and watched a paper die. We waited in the home of a man who once had run it. A flash came over the phone. The *World* was ended.

F. P. A. looked eagerly at a bowl of fruit upon the table and said, "Mr. Swope, where have you been buying your apples?"

I've opposed the theories of those who would break up mergers, end chain stores and try the trick of unscrambling large-scale production. I've said that this could not be done —that it wasn't even expedient. In the long run the happiness of all of us depends upon increased efficiency and a shorter sum of toil. That's true. I still believe it. I wouldn't weep about a shoe factory or a branch-line railroad shutting down.

But newspapers are different. I'm a news-paperman. There are many things to be said for this new combination. It is my sincere belief that the Scripps-Howard chain is qualified by its record and its potentialities to carry on the Pulitzer tradition of liberal journalism.

Yet I hope at least that this may be the end of mergers. The economic pressure for consolidation still continues. A newspaper is, among other things, a business. And, even so, it must be more than that. A lawyer at the hearing before Surrogate Foley expressed amazement that a paper which had lost almost $2,000,000 within a year could command any of that intangible value known as "good will." He was reasoning from the basis upon which fish are canned and wire wheels turned out.

A newspaper is a rule unto itself. It has a soul for salvation or damnation. I was pleased to hear much said about intangibles in all the accounts of the preliminary negotiations leading up to the present merger. I was glad that for once the emphasis was taken away from mere machinery. The fact of presses and lino-type equipment was never stressed in the proceedings. This didn't count. The intangibles

of a newspaper are the men and the women
who make it.

First in America, and now in a frenzied form
in Russia, there grows a cult which bows and
bangs its head upon the floor in worship of
the machine. In some calculations man is no
more than a device to pull upon a gadget. But
here, at last, there was talk of millions, and
checks in huge amounts were passed—not for
apparatus, moving belts, and intricate mecha-
nism. This was a deal for a name and for some
of the people who contributed to the making
of the name.

Since my feeling is strong that a newspaper
can neither rise nor fall beyond or below its
staff, I was stirred by the notion—the dream
—that *World* men might take over the *World*.
I realize, as they do now, the difficulties which
lay in the path of any such plan. I'll readily
admit that 1,000 to 1 would be a generous
price against any such undertaking. But we
are, or ought to be, lovers of long-shots.
There's nothing particularly stirring when the
favorite coasts home in front. Although the
newspaper crowd didn't put their project
over, it isn't fair to call this miss plain failure.

For almost the first time in my life I watched reporters animated by a group consciousness. Newspapermen are blandly and, I think, blindly individualistic. Once I was president of a press-writers' union. There were four members. The three others were the secretary, the vice-president, and the treasurer. The treasurer never had much responsibility. Nobody would join us, because the average reporter carried in his knapsack the baton of a managing editor, or even the dim hope of being some day a dramatic critic. What did he want with organization? He stood on two feet—a single unit.

But for a time down in the *World* office there was the excitement, the hip-hip-hooray, call it even the hysteria of mob movement, of people rubbing shoulders and saying, "We are in this boat together."

One of the things which would have made the fruition of the plan extremely difficult is the fact that a paper lives or dies by personality. When forty or fifty are banded together they must select a single one to be the leader and articulate representative. Still, in any dream of a coöperative commonwealth I've always had the feeling that newspapers most of all were fit subjects for some sort of socialization. I've never known even the most obscure reporter who didn't think he knew more about running a paper than the man who owned it. I've always felt that way myself. And once I was right.

The curious thing concerning the death of the *World* was the manner in which it became animate just before the final rattle within its throat. Within the last two or three years there must have been times in which the morale of the staff was low. The last night I went late to see the men I knew and had worked with long ago—that is, two years, or maybe three, which is a long span in the life of any roving and rebellious columnist. I never found the paper pounding and pulsing quite so much as it did now—when it was dead.

We sat together in a very vigorous sort of democracy. At first I felt I might be out of place as one who was an ex-*World* man. But by four in the morning we were all "ex." We had ex-managing editor, ex-city editor, and dozens of ex-reporters. For the first time within

many months it was possible for somebody
who covered a district to point the finger of
scorn or accusation at somebody who had been
his boss and spill his whole mind and emotion.
You didn't have to "sir" anybody or say "very
good" or "yes" unless you wanted to. Out of
a situation which was certainly tragic to many
there was at least a glimpse of that heaven in
which we may all walk and between harp
tunes look up and say with impunity to any
passing angel or archangel, "Oh, is that so?"

Naturally, I have both hope and confidence
in the new paper. Like John Brown's body, the
World goes marching on. To heights, I hope.
But something is gone. They aren't all marching. Men have dropped out. For them there
will be nothing more on any newspaper, and I
think of these casualties. I think of a profession which grows efficient and overcrowded.
And to those who can no longer make the
grade and who stand under the indictment of
being not good enough I bow low, I swing my
hat, as if it bore a plume, and say:

"Good, bad, or indifferent, you have been
in it. You belong. Some part of stuff set down
on paper was you, and ever will be."

The ship-news reporter of the World *had to be on a vacation cruise when everything happened. He tells about losing a job overboard.*

JUST BREAK THE NEWS

By John T. Parker, Jr.

Ship-News Reporter

THE sun shone brightly, bands played, and men and women cheered and waved as the brave ship sailed away.

As a ship-news reporter, maritime affairs, it may seem quite natural, have occupied at least some of my time. Perhaps more than a considerate but suspicious city editor might care to believe. But the point in mind is that original lead to this slight essay. Look back on all maritime disasters—the *Titanic*, the *Vestris*, etc. Why, of course you remember! When they sailed—it always appeared this way—the bands had played, that same old bright sun had shone, and the conventional men and women, apparently always on hand for such impending tragedies, had done the same cheering and waving.

So it was when I sailed away for a cruise to the West Indies aboard the Cosulich liner *Vulcania*. The date, for those interested in figures, happened to be the 17th of February. And again to refer to those sad affairs of the sea, no one dreamed of the impending tragedy.

But to correct any impression before it is too late, nothing, by the way, happened to the good *Vulcania*. The entire maritime disaster was strictly localized to one of its passengers, your correspondent, personally and pointedly.

To be sure, about the time of my departure there had appeared a cloud on the horizon, but no bigger than a man's hand, I believe the expression goes. This hand, incidently, happened to belong to one Walter Winchell, who had been impudent enough to keep suggesting that the *World* would be sold. His boldness had proceeded to such lengths that he had even stated it would be sold to the Scripps-Howard organization—this several months before the personal maritime disaster I am about both to experience and to relate. Of course, Winchell was soundly trounced and

properly punished for his *lèse majesté*. At once
there appeared on the bulletin board of the
World a notice that no one on the staff of the
paper was to supply the rogue with any information. The following day Winchell printed
this notice.

At the time, no one, of course—including
probably, Ralph E. Renaud, managing editor
and author of the note—appreciated this high
touch of the sardonic. Any member of the staff
who might have supplied Winchell with this
information—up to and including the date of
the appearance of the brothers Pulitzer before
Surrogate Foley—has apparently kept his
word to carry the secret to his grave.

So I made my departure, secure in the impending voyage of the *Vulcania* as I was in the
future course of the *World*. Well, that is, I did
know the *Vulcania* would be out for twenty-
one days. The owners of the Cosulich line
bravely made no secret about this matter and
sold passages accordingly.

On Tuesday at 2 P.M.—this date will be
referred to in other parts of this volume—a
dramatic incident occurred to this member of
the *World's* staff—an altogether electrifying

event. I discovered by direct and first-hand knowledge that a bottle of Black Label Johnny Walker could be purchased in Willemsted, Curaçoa for $2.20. This, I recalled, was cheaper even than England, Curaçoa being a free port. As I wonderingly had the bottle wrapped—merely for the scientific proof in future of such a phenomenon—I was probably too absorbed to wonder what the boys back home were doing. I'm not sure, but I guess I was. If I had stopped to think, I might have seen Allen Norton pause at Racky's on his way to the Federal Building and pay his tribute, in much greater gold, to Prohibition.

As we had been in port, no radio news had been received by the ship. This news—three pages, single spaces, was received from Associated Press during the early morning and, through the kindness of the *Vulcania's* radio staff, brought to my cabin at eight o'clock every morning. There had been none on Tuesday, as I recall, and, as we had left port quite late, none the following day.

On Wednesday, the *Vulcania* logged along at a fast clip through a beautiful blue sea. The sun was quite bright and warm—just a cinch to be lazy. Sitting in this sun in a bathing-suit seemed a good idea at the time, being just mean enough to think back to the city room with the gleeful thought that while some were sure to be sitting around the city room, feeling just as lazy, they didn't have the same sun or the bathing-suit—merely Jim Barrett, sure to be worrying about the Bank of United States story. I was sure that story would still be running.

We reached Kingston, Jamaica, B. W. I., early next morning. About 11 A.M. that morning I was confronted with an important decision. I thought, too, at that moment, with a deserted city room Alex Schlosser would also be confronted with an important decision—perhaps just what reporter he would telephone and get out of bed to cover the birth of a new giraffe at the Bronx Zoo. My decision was much more complex, I was certain at the moment, than any that might be confronting anyone on Park Row.

The problem, and its ultimate decision, was purely personal. I knew that if I walked a few hot, dusty, and windy blocks, I would reach the Hotel Myrtlebank, where in a cool grove, shaded by tall palms, lay the best mint julep still to be obtained in the Western Hemisphere. But then, it was early in the day, the sun was broiling hot—and mint juleps are great time-savers. After all, I had a full day in port. With a certain high moral self-satisfaction I elected to stay aboard the *Vulcania*.

At 2 P.M. I made a tentative decision, but no public announcement—this merely be-cause most of my fellow passengers were amus-ing themselves with a long, hot, and dusty as well as tiring automobile ride somewhere or other. I went ashore and strolled gently and leisurely under a hot sun to the Myrtlebank. There, as breezes swept through palms and became cool in the shade, I had a good long mint julep with frost thick and steaming on the glass. I paused for the contemplative and slightly malicious thought as to whether my co-workers in the city room were just as happy —and in as true a sense of the word. I have since learned this was not so—which, by the way, goes for both, if I had any of the informa-tion they had, or did not have.

This was for me an exhausting day—as can be plainly seen from the multitude of deci-

sions. At 7 P.M. I knew I was just as rushed as
anyone that moment in the city room. If Ben
Franklin had his worries at the moment—
whether to order a No. 1 or a top of a 10 on
that taxi smash-up, I had my worries at the
moment whether or not Mrs. B ——— then on
a shore excursion, would want to dress for the
dinner we were to have at the Myrtlebank. We
dressed for dinner, although I had no idea
what Ben Franklin did about that story.

Then at midnight it took me a long time to
decide whether or not a brandy flip would
serve as a good-nightcap on top of all those
mint juleps and planters' punches. It did, and
so, exhausted, I went to bed.

We sailed that night from Kingston, and
next morning I awoke. There is nothing new
or strange in that simple statement except that
some awakenings are brighter and clearer
than others. The one in question was the re-
verse of a movie fade-out. With no sudden
moves or jarring sounds, I slowly faded in and
picked up the radio news that had been delivered to my cabin.

Oh yes, there was something at first about
Hoover and Congress; there generally was.

Ghandi and the French-Italian naval pact came next, some New York vice stuff, and then —the *World* had been sold! I woke up.

This was just great. What was it all about? I read the three or four lines about twenty times, hoping that those words between the lines would appear. The message was painfully brief and exasperatingly cloudy. It did not quite make clear what had happened. I was sure the man filing the radio stuff in New York knew what it meant—I knew he must have columns of news before him to get the stuff. But this—it was clear that the paper had been sold. Scripps-Howard—yes, Winchell had mentioned that. But what, just what had happened?

What had preceded this? How was this sudden sale possible? What had happened to the staff? Who else had tried to buy it, and had anything drastic happened to cause this? Mixed with my wonder was a good amount of anger that my various superiors had allowed me to go on vacation—so far from the scene of action—without a hint other than the rumors I knew we all knew.

Cheer was hardly the word to describe my

somewhat disorganized feelings at this point. To a New York lady I happened to know on board I mentioned, as casually as I could, that the *World* had been sold.

"Oh, that's fine!" she said. "That will give me one less paper to buy on Sunday."

This helped!

Still only vaguely aware of the events of the sale and the future outcome of the paper, I went ashore as soon as we reached Havana on Saturday. At the gate of the pier I bought a *World* and a *Herald Tribune.* This provided just another touch—it was Wednesday's *World* and Thursday's *Herald Tribune.* Then, like listening to Alice in Wonderland's Red Queen describe a train wreck, I started with Wednesday's paper to read about what was happening. That is, I knew in a vague way what had happened—not exactly—and here I was, days behind, reading the events leading to the thing that had happened. On Sunday I got Friday's *Herald Tribune* and a play-by-play account of the bad news. On Monday, Charles F. Noyes, who had flown to Miami and back, brought copies of the *New York Times* from Thursday to Sunday. Then I was able to see in more detail how publishers do their own handwriting on the wall.

The feeling of being so far away and help-less about such events—of course, I did not know then that the latter feeling had nothing to do with distance—was far from a source of comfort. I suppose, though, a truer statement would be that any newspaperman likes to be where things are happening, even though there is nothing he can do about them—or, as is fre-quently the case—is supposed to do about them.

Then, the lack of knowledge of the personal element was a cause of concern. The various editors and reporters I had worked with for six years—what would happen to them? With no chance of getting back for several days, be-sides the concern for them, it is only correct to say that I reserved some part of this con-cern for personal use.

And so I sailed back to New York, perhaps the last of the staff to return, arriving eight days after the sale. So far I have seen but two members of the staffs of the *World* and *Eve-*

ning World to gather somewhere and discuss the events leading up to the tragedy. But I'll probably meet up with them sooner or later. Because, even as the youngest Pulitzer might observe, it's a small world, after all.

We may as well confess it—Elsie McCormick was assigned to do the "woman's angle" on the end of the World. That is almost as bad as asking her to give us on the same object "A piece of her mind."

DOOMSDAY

By Elsie McCormick

NOBODY who was on the staff can ever forget the poignant emotional quality of the last day of the *New York World*.

There had been, on Tuesday afternoon, the shock of the first report, followed by waves of consternation and unbelief. The initial story of the petition had gone around the building with the crackling speed of a prairie fire. Men and women poured into the city room from all departments, forming into groups that buzzed with the incredible news.

Perhaps the most vivid mental picture of that day is of long rows of people sitting on the desks. Somehow, to sit on a desk and dangle one's feet gives a certain mental assurance—a feeling of being at ease and unafraid.

Then there was the high hope of the days when the employees believed that they might buy the *World* out of their own capital. When I reached the office on Wednesday morning, petitions asking the court for time to raise the money were being circulated by reporters in the city room.

Those signing were warned that, in case the paper was sold, they ran the possible risk of being deprived of the usual two weeks' salary and perhaps of being blacklisted by the new consolidated journal. Outside of those bound by contracts, only two on the editorial staff failed to sign their names.

There were two days during which a spirit of self-sacrifice swept over the building like a fiery cloud. The paper suddenly became personalized; its death agonies were as poignant as those of a dearly beloved relative. The first thought of everyone on the staff was to save it, by no matter what sacrifice to himself.

On the second morning two adding-machines were set up in the city room to count the subscriptions that poured in from all the staff. Crowded among my memories of that day are copy boys offering fifty dollars each, a worker from the composing-room signing up for a thousand dollars, and a delegation from the mailing department coming in to offer their savings to the committee.

For a time the staff seemed to be living through a war and a revolution rolled into one. Every notice on the bulletin board drew an anxious crowd of fifty or sixty people, as excited as civilians reading dispatches from the front.

Deputations in overalls came down to the city room and joined in the councils of the editorial group. The signs posted about the building asked that subscriptions be made to the "central committee" of each department, a phrase that was unintentionally Russian and that increased the resemblance to a Soviet.

Everyone seemed reluctant to leave the building. Men off duty joined the crowds around the bulletin board. In fact, there was little inclination to go out even during the lunch hour. The rather dingy restaurant upstairs, generally patronized only on rainy days, all at once became a sentimental shrine.

As the hours went by, the employees felt a great increase in confidence. Subscriptions for $600,000 were already in hand, and pledges were coming in from all over the country. Everyone seemed to believe that an unknown savior would gallop up at the last minute and offer bags of gold to the committee. If only final action could be long enough delayed, the *New York World* would belong to its employees.

When I left the paper early on Thursday afternoon, the office was still bright with an air of hope. Subscriptions and encouraging telegrams were pouring in, and everybody seemed to hear the off-stage approach of a mysterious Midas on horseback.

When I returned at about ten o'clock that night there had been a marked change. A feeling of hopelessness, a hint of death, was discernible as soon as one left the elevator. Except the few reporters then out on assignments, practically all the editorial staff was crowded into the city room. Mingling with them were a few outside friends, some old members of the *World* alumni, and an ominous number of reporters from other papers, sent in to cover the death watch.

The decision, we had heard, was to come at eleven o'clock. As the hour approached, the atmosphere in the crowded city room became almost unbearably tense. The staff watched the clock like condemned men, jumping concertedly every time the telephone rang and crowding around to listen to the conversation. For a time one was reminded forcibly of the deathhouse scene in "The Last Mile."

Eleven o'clock passed without word. The tension grew greater, false rumors rippling over the room at the rate of one every five minutes. People crowded around the dais of the day city editor and the night desk alternately, pursuing the whisper that word had arrived at last.

It was twelve thirty o'clock when the first news of the decision came over the telephone. There were a few moments of dazed unbelief; then a reporter, with face as strained as that of the runner from the battle of Marathon, rushed in with the photostatic copy.

Clustered around the copy desk, a hundred people elbowed one another as they struggled to read the document. Rank and discipline

235

were entirely forgotten—an office boy dug his chin into the shoulder of the managing editor as he stared in fascination at the white-lettered sheets.

People who could not possibly scan the long report hung breathlessly over the desk while the sheets were being "slugged" and headed and passed to the copy-reader. The crowd followed the progress of each page with the wide-eyed wonder of children at a conjuror's show, unable to believe what was passing before their eyes. Almost the only sound in the room was the clicking of Lindesay Parrott's typewriter as he wrote the story of the paper's last hours.

After the decision had gone up to the composing-room, the crowd flocked around Mr. Barrett's desk again while a last appeal was drafted and sent to the Pulitzers. Permission to sell did not necessarily mean that the paper was sold; if the owners would grant the employees only forty-eight hours, there was still hope that the *World* might be saved.

But no reply came. A telephone call to Herbert Pulitzer and a plea that the employees be at least relieved of their agonizing suspense brought only a non-committal response from his polished English secretary. In a short time two typewritten statements came, announcing that the sale had been made and that the *World* was suspending immediately.

The result was a strange release of pent-up feeling. Men who had not slept in seventy-two hours suddenly began to laugh. A group of sixty or seventy gathered around the city editor's desk and burst into "Hail, hail, the gang's all here," coming down with especially vivid emphasis on, "What the hell do we care now?"

Then, swelling into a great chorus that almost lifted the dome, the voices of editors, reporters, and copy boys joined in singing, "J. P.'s body lies a-mouldering in the grave, but his soul goes marching on." One wrought-up reporter suggested that the entire party start on a taxicab pilgrimage to Joseph Pulitzer's burial-place. The idea, however, was vetoed.

This marked the high emotional peak of the evening—at least the peak of obvious emotion. The rest of the songs included a hearty rendering of "Ach, du lieber Pulitzers, Pulitzers, Pulitzers," and a ballad of many verses concerning the activities of Chile Acuna, many lines of which were given merely as "Tra, la, la" in deference to the more or less restraining presence of the ladies of the staff.

Some toasts were drunk from paper cups, and a few gentle blessings called down upon the heads of Herbert, Ralph, and the Junior Joseph.

Upstairs the compositors, some of whom had been with the paper for forty years, were standing among the linotype machines and singing the words of "Auld Lang Syne."

After the last edition had gone to bed, the crowd in the morning city room began to break up. Some of the group drifted out to continue the wake in different surroundings, but others, unable still to believe that the paper was gone, stayed on until dawn came in through the tall, murky windows.

The death of the *World* proved to be slow and long drawn out. Next day, when a solemn and tired-eyed group gathered in the city room, the facetiousness of the night before was gone. Reporters sat on the closed desks and dangled their feet, staring dazedly at the bouquets of red tulips that stood before the places of the day and night editors.

At one o'clock the room was thronged by a thousand employees. Men and women struggled for standing room on the desks and packed themselves breathlessly into the narrow aisles. Jim Barrett outlined to them the possibilities of starting a new coöperative paper on the ashes of the old *World*, and there was an attempt to put through a resolution calling for its establishment.

Several staff members offered informally to give their services for thirty-five dollars a week. An announcement that F. P. A. had volunteered to work three months without salary brought a round of applause.

But the high, hopeful spirit of the previous two days was gone. The crowd seemed to realize that it was beaten and that it was making its last forlorn gesture. When a gold watch was presented to Mr. Barrett and he held it up, unable to speak, a number of the staff unashamedly gave way to tears.

For several days after that *World* employees

THE END OF THE WORLD

came back again and again to loiter in the quiet city room. But the silence and the slow dismantlement became more than they could bear, and the room was left at last to the memories of other days.

Read the story of what happened in the troubled soul of the Art Department as its patron—the whole World—lay dying.

PORTRAIT OF THE ARTIST AS A CORPSE

By Leo Kober

ON THE 26th of February, 1931, around 2:30 P.M., Phil Stong's ever-smiling round face appeared at the door of the Sunday Art. How on that day a person was able to smile was more than I ever will understand. But, then again, not being an American by birth, the ever-smiling process of "what's the use of worrying" is by no means part of my gamut. But Phil did smile, as usual. And in his raised hand he waved what I knew was a story for the Sunday editorial. And it meant me. I was to make a picture for it.

Now that my last week's salary and the two weeks of grace have been paid off to me, I might as well confess that up to that minute I hadn't done a stroke of work all week, and

241

this was Thursday. Nobody had. Since Monday morning we had been in the rumor business, working up, chewing, digesting or rather trying to digest, rumors. You can't set your mind on drawing pictures if you are knocked over by rumors. The only busy guy around our place was Sammy. The whole week he was busy running around diving into mysterious channels for inside info', also consulting lawyers, district attorneys, and court attendants. As an orderly citizen he wanted to face the music with a legally set mind. He was busy as hell. But the rest of us, including the boss—*nolens, volens*—preferred the rumor business.

Smiling Phil handed me the story, and it was about Mr. Hoover. In my six years of service in the Sunday Art up to this day I had read in the neighborhood of about one thousand stories or so which were given to me to illustrate. And I had always read them rather carefully. And with this one, too, I sat down to read it. Somehow I only saw typewritten letters dancing in front of my eyes. All I could gather from the ten-page manuscript was that it was on President Hoover and that

242

Mr. Hoover wasn't so happy those days, after all. But neither was I, I thought. The *World* was toppling down over my head, so why should I be interested in Mr. Hoover's happiness. It probably was an excellent story with a lot of good lines for a cartoon, only I couldn't find them. So when it came down to brass tacks, which means "go ahead with that two-column," I did what in those six years I had done so often, if for some reason or other no picture idea offered itself immediately—I suggested to Michelson, or Mike, as we called him, that the best and only thing to do was a straight portrait of the President. If an artist is out of ideas, a straight portrait is always the thing. Mike said "Yaus," which in I don't know what language meant O. K. with Mike.

When I started my straight portrait of Mr. Hoover, Bob Ament, the art boss, came up to my desk and looked over my shoulder.

"What's that?" he asked.

"Sunday editorial," I said.

To me Bob Ament, besides being the boss, ever meant the reincarnation of Voltaire's

"Candide ou l'Optimisme." In the face of an earthquake, I think, Bob was the guy to say this: "Wait a minute; don't run! It might be one of those quakes where ruins don't come down but are shooting up to heaven." No such earthquakes were ever known to anybody, but Bob was the man to trust that there might be earthquakes of that kind. So when he saw me working again, he triumphantly said:

"Didn't I tell you, boys? In ten years from now I still will be standing behind Leo's back and tell him, 'For Christ's sake, can't you get some more action into that thing?' " . . .

Losing hope was a thing unknown to Bob Ament. So on the 26th of February at 3 P.M. he still was full of hope. And hope it was, real hope. Not our kind of hope that was the hope of the crew of a sinking ship, hope that they wouldn't be drowned and that they might save their lives somehow. He still believed in the ship. He was a great hoper, Bob was!

"Will there ever be another Sunday paper, you think?" I asked.

He only laughed.

"Remember, in ten years from now . . .

But this time Candide had missed his guess . . .

Sammy came dashing in from another conference with the coroner.

"What's the latest?" he was greeted.

"Court's decision at five-thirty," said Sammy, registering utmost well-informedness. His face looked like a murder headline.

"Who told you?"

"I have it from a very reliable source," said Sammy, mysteriously.

"Those front-elevator guys don't know a thing!" remarked Herb Roth. "I've just talked to Charley in the tower elevator; he says it will be at five-forty-three . . ."

By the time I'd gotten through with Mr. Hoover, around four, the big Sunday room was a madhouse.

Ties of office discipline were gone, official standings obliterated. It was that real democracy that comes with trouble. Mary Davis was involved in a heated conversation with the office boys. Henry Tyrell and Willy Laas were wildly interpreting old Mr. Joseph Pulitzer's will. Rody Butterworth was trying hard to pull lovely Miss Shapiro out of a sort of deep coma, while Jim of the composing-room went around asking everybody, as usual, "How are yah makin' out?" getting replies of very different shades. Out of Mike's room came the hollering laughter of Bob, who made it his business to cheer up people. . . . I had the idea that he was like a nurse among the sick in a lunatic asylum . . . Herb Roth gave Sammy a tarty lecture on the Code Napoleon, while impassibly, like the veiled idol of Saïs, Earl Eisfeller was sitting at his desk, staring out of the window at the top of the Woolworth tower, as if Surrogate Foley were sitting up there, ready to let him know his decision by flag signals. Telephones were ringing, bringing or asking for "the latest." Some very courageous soul—I think it was Liebling, the Bald,—sat still pounding away on a typewriter. In the air was grim humor—the scaffold kind—and sighs of resignation. And behind it all one thought . . . can it be??? . . .

Down City Hall Park, in the purplish foggy light the crowd of home-rushing office-workers, the endless stream of automobiles, honking, tooting, belching, and the unfailable roar of

the bell of some hook-and-ladder. . . . Yes,
life will go on as usual, while up here a world
was dying. . . .

"Decision of the Court will be handed down
at six," it came.

With Bob, Mike, and Paul Sifton we went
over to the Hall of Records. Surrounded by
eager reporters from other papers—we meant
news to them this time!—we were pacing the
dignified corridors for another hour. Then it
was said, "Not before eight." Then again, at
ten-thirty or later . . . around midnight, perhaps. . . .

Around eleven every living soul had gathered in the big city room on the twelfth. What
happened there is related in this book by more
qualified pens than mine. . . . For some reason—was it to be prepared for everything?—
I needed a clean handkerchief. There was one
in my coat which I had left in the Sunday room
down on the eleventh. So down I went and
stepped into the "Sunday Art Department."

The big room was empty and pitch dark.
It struck me that somewhere around Earl's

desk there lay or stood something that, like a
streak of lightning, stood out in the darkness,
like a flash of a glaring, stretched light. It was,
it turned out, a big T-square that was reflecting some light which came I don't know from
where. It was very childish, but at this
moment I thought, Is it a flash of hope? . . .
I did not feel ashamed of my childishness that
moment. I think I never will. . . .

. . . Here they were, Bob's desk and
Herb's desk and Sammy's desk and Earl's
desk and Jack's desk and mine. "Sunday Art
Department" . . . an office for Art, the daily
rendezvous place of a few men with the Muses,
for circulation-raising purposes. . . .

What a joke it sounds like! And yet the holy
flame of true enthusiasm, the eternal light of
big doings, here in this room it was kept going
and burning. How they looked in print! . . .
Who cares? Daily hackwork and . . . beating, throbbing, struggling hearts of artists
with the everlasting, never-ceasing side glance
for the great and the beautiful. . . . Art, to
live only one short day; Art, enchained into
two columns and three columns, veloxes and

silverprints, comics, pretty girls and cartoons
. . . done by men devoted to a great and
wonderful passion. Passion transposed into
jobs, holy struggle into daily routine, but passion and struggling still . . . the great dashing desire of creation, cut into pieces, for Sunday morning use, as accompaniment of the
breakfast coffee with pancakes . . . but still
the great, imperative desire. . . .

All this, with the glaring flash of the T-
square, was shining through the darkness, between old desks, pieces of torn paper, latest
editions, telephones, and waste-baskets. . . .

And across the street, in the Hall of Records, the death sentence was being pronounced. All this was to die, to be shot at
sunrise, years of hard work to be wiped out,
become souvenirs.

"In ten years from now . . ."
Candide had missed his guess this time.

How long I had been sitting there I don't
know. What finally woke me up was the shrill
ring of the telephone on Bob's desk. But I
decided to commit my first act of violation of

office discipline and not to answer it. The Sunday Art had died, I decided, and it had.

Up on the twelfth floor people were waiting. Groups, hanging together like grapes on one stem, they were sitting, standing, leaning, lying on desks over typewriters, smiling smiles of consternation, but still smiles. On one desk, right on top of it, facing Barrett's, a little hunchbacked dwarf was sitting, and he too was smiling. . . .

From the far end of the tremendous room a man in shirt sleeves was working his way through the crowd. In his hand he held a piece of paper. They barred his way. He had run them over as he headed for Barrett's desk. . . .

Then a few hoarse words came out of his throat. . . .

". . . Flash. . . . Foley permits sale. . . ."

Did he say "Flash"?

Yes, it was the flash of the T-square down there.

Candide had missed his guess. Mr. Hoover's straight portrait never saw the sunlight of another Sunday. . . .

Sunday Art was no more.

A lawyer is given thirty minutes' notice to save a newspaper.

SOME LEGAL ASPECTS

By Gustavus A. Rogers

Attorney for the World Employees

THE legal aspect of the "end of the *World*" has a point of humor as well as its serious side.

About two minutes before one, on the afternoon of February 25th, I received a telephone call inviting me to represent the employees of the *World* publications, at a hearing scheduled before Surrogate James A. Foley, at 1:30 that afternoon (only thirty-two minutes subsequent to the telephone call). Preparation for the argument was to be made after my arrival at court; the distance I was obliged to travel from my office to the courthouse was about three miles. Resorting to a ride by Subway, I arrived at court about 1:25. Fortunately, since the proceedings were a trifle late in starting, I had the benefit of a *ten-minute* conference with my principal client, James W. Barrett,

251

city editor of the *World*. I had not seen at that time, nor in fact for several hours after the hearing had been concluded, the last will and testament of Joseph Pulitzer, the document before the court for its construction.

I had erroneously concluded from the recital to me that none of the employees were in court as a matter of right; in any event, I had no present information on which to base the claim of such a legal status as would justify their intervention in the proceedings without permission of the Court; it seemed to me that only as *amicus curia* ("a friend of the court") could they be heard.

It was represented to me that there was possibility, if the proceedings were delayed or postponed a fortnight, that the employees would be enabled to present an offer to acquire the "intangibles" and for which, I was informed, Roy Howard, of the Scripps-Howard publications, had submitted a bid; accordingly, I requested a postponement of further proceedings.

I had not at that time seen any of the documents, and even at this time we have not been permitted to see a copy of what is denominated the contract, for the purchase of the "intangibles," generally consisting of the names *The World, Evening World,* and *Sunday World,* together with the memberships of these papers in the Associated Press.

We were most graciously received by the Court, and as the counsel for the employees I was not only permitted to address the Court, but also invited by Surrogate Foley to join in the conference of the attorneys representing the various interests, which, at the request of the counsel for the interested parties, was to be in closed session rather than in public.

The proceedings were concluded some time after three o'clock. The Court instructed the counsel for the trustees of the Pulitzer estate to supply me with a copy of the will; having obtained this, I also obtained the minutes of the hearing of the previous day. Upon an examination, we discovered that there is a provision of the will denominated Article VI, clause 6, which reads as follows:

(6) As to the remaining one-tenth (1/10) portion of the stock of the said two Companies bequeathed in trust to my Executors, other than the Union Trust Company, I direct my said Trustees

to distribute the income thereof during the continuance of the "trust term" hereinbefore provided for by clauses (1) and (5) of this Article among those of the principal Editors and Managers of said newspapers whom my said Trustees may regard as most deserving and valuable to said newspapers, from time to time, and upon the expiration of the trust estate, said one-tenth (1/10) of said stock of each of said Companies shall be sold on such liberal terms as my Executors may think best, to one of the principal Editors or Managers of each of said newspapers respectively, whom my Trustees may consider most deserving in point of ability and integrity.

The concluding portion of the paragraph was by codicil executed May 11, 1910, modified so that it shall be *"one or more"* instead of *"only one"* of the principal editors or managers of the *World* and *Post Dispatch.*

Having concluded that because of the provisions of the will the "principal editors and managers" had the direct interest of being practically one-tenth partners in the newspaper enterprise, we filed on their behalf a notice of appearance by James W. Barrett, the city editor, and Foster Gilroy, assistant business manager of the *World*, in a representative capacity,—*i.e.*, on behalf of all the editors and managers, coupled with the request that we be permitted to adduce testimony and file a brief.

The Surrogate evidently concluded that while we had some rights in the matter, it was not involved in the proceedings before him and these he reserved for adjudication by a supplemental decree; the correctness of his pronouncement is challenged by us and will probably be presented to an appellate tribunal for review, in this instance the Appellate Division of the Supreme Court.

The Surrogate subsequently, and at about midnight of February 25th, handed down an opinion, which in effect construed the will as being elastic and that a sale could be had of the *World* newspaper "intangibles" in an emergency, even though by direct language of the will such a result was practically forbidden by the testator. The opinion of Judge Foley is a classic upon the subject, even though there may be legal minds differing from the soundness of the views he expressed.

It is a matter of common knowledge that, although the Surrogate directed that the decree, which was to be entered following his opinion, was to be "settled on notice" to the counsel for the interested parties, without the formality of entering the decree and within two hours after it was handed down, the trustees and the officers of the Press Publishing Company proceeded to carry the contract to full performance and scrapped the newspapers. The propriety, if not the legality, of such procedure, to the mind of the writer, is one upon which much might be said: there is strong probability that the matter will be the subject of future adjudication by the Court. In any event, the question is open to whether a valid decree can be entered under the circumstances in the absence of and representation by "the principal editors and managers."

The well-known literary editor who conducted the World's *First Reader Column writes a chapter without first having read a book.*

THE LAST READER

By Harry Hansen

WHEN I came to the *World* the Quarter Century Club had just elected William Johnston to membership, and he remarked that I still had a long road to travel before I would be entitled to sit at dinner with the men who remembered the voice of the elder Pulitzer. Herbert Bayard Swope took me up into the Dome to the office of the publisher, by way of the famous elevator that I had heard described so often. As we came out after I had received my appointment from Ralph Pulitzer I said to Swope that I hoped that I should be with the *World* for many years; he added that he hoped I would. My remark expressed my emotion at finally joining the staff of the newspaper that had such an enviable name in American journalism.

Bill Johnston had suggested me; he was, in fact, suggestion editor, a title which, he explained, had grown out of the fact that nobody knew exactly what to call him. Editors rarely took any suggestions, he said, but for some strange reason they accepted me. He was a man with an extraordinary capacity for friendship. Nothing that he did had any relation to a possible future repayment to his advantage. In a world in which men either pursue their own fortunes avidly without regard for those around them, or in the heat of competition push their fellow men aside, Bill Johnston was an anomaly. He was always cheerful, always helpful, never too hurried to go out of his way to do a kindness. He had learned, early in life, that nothing else really pays. It may be well that he did not see the end of the *World*. Despite his realistic attitude toward it, his completely objective estimates of the men who made it, he regarded it as a fixed star for men to steer by.

It was through Johnston's kind office that I had an interview with Ralph Pulitzer and met Swope. Although I was a citizen of no mean city, and for a long time had been associated with newspapermen who took no lead from the *World*, or, for that matter, from anyone, I confess that my first visit to the office of the executive editor was high adventure. In that room up among the cornices, overlooking the diminutive City Hall, staring out past the Woolworth tower toward the river where ships moved into port, I found myself reflecting on the fortunes of men. At the hour of five Swope was in action. And with the true instinct of the publicist he tolerated no secrets in his presence. What he had to say all the town might hear; what he did all the town might see. Men walked in and out of his private office; he introduced them and continued talking. Sometimes he shot a question into space and received an answer from the more deliberate and balanced Bill Beazell just on the other side of the partition. Alexander Woollcott strolled in to exchange a few words on the acting of Alice Brady; Swope had. seen the opening. Louis Weitzenkorn interrupted with his direct and business-like, "I say, boss . . ." "Meet Milt Gross," said Swope. "He's just been out on the Coast. How'd you get along with Charlie, Milt?" "He and I are just like that," said

Milt, shaking hands with himself. Nize Baby was the sensation of New York. "Why can't they sell it in Chicago?" asked Swope. And I thought of the Babel of tongues on Maxwell Street and wondered. When the publisher himself entered the room there was no change in attitude. "Hello, Ralph!" said Swope . . . and Ralph and Aleck began examining a new pipe. In Chicago we had mentioned the publisher only in subdued tones; we had approached his presence with a prayer.

The great days, I was given to understand, had been firmly established. The talk of the town had been led by Deems Taylor, Alexander Woollcott, Heywood Broun, Laurence Stallings, and F. P. A. Stallings had built himself up into a powerful writer; other opportunities now took his time and he was slowly slipping out from under the newspaper harness. It had become necessary to get a successor. New York was full of hopefuls and possibilities, but for some reason the *World* turned to Chicago. That meant a change in my fortunes which was much more important to me than it can ever have been to the *World*. I was faced, however, with uprooting myself completely from the Middle West with which I had identified myself. I did not know then, as I do now, that New York City was Paducah, and Chillicothe, and Springfield and Cedar Rapids, and all the milkstops from here to Kalamazoo. "If you are ever coming to New York," said J. F. Bresnahan the day I sat with him and F. D. White at the Hardware Club, "I should think that now is the time." . . . "It would be fatal to leave Chicago," cautioned a New York friend who had his own candidate. "Remember, there you're the big frog in that puddle, whereas here. . . ." The inference was easy. I came. "May the *World* be your oyster!" wrote Christopher Morley, in greeting.

The theory that books are news is anathema to some critics and philosophers; I have seen it condemned as the consuming evil of modern writing. Yet books have always been news and men have told about them breathlessly, whether discoursing on the historical exactness of Thucydides or discovering merits in Goldsmith's latest comedy in eighteenth-century London. In our own day the aloof thinker is almost unknown; the activities of our age

impinge upon our time, worldly events ferret
us out, even in our homes and hillside retreats.
Half the books published are properly records
of events, only partly transmuted; expository
writing has a tremendous vogue; the preoccu-
pation with underlying ideas is slight. If readers were eager to hear about the latest
biography, to become acquainted with the latest novel, surely the newspaper was a suitable
medium of communication.

There are two ways of doing this: one by
giving a gorgeous show, an entertainment in
which the book is the excuse; the other by taking for granted that the reader is more interested in the book than in the man who reviews
it. The *World's* great page was built on the
first practice; Woollcott, F. P. A., Stallings
were great medicine-men, prestidigitators;
Taylor was more likely to keep himself in the
background. What Stallings had done with
The First Reader was still vivid in my memory; my child had been among the slain. He
was a two-gun man, quick on the trigger; in
his belt he carried a cutlass with a razor-edge
for use when his cartridges stuck. I was doubt-
ful whether the readers of "the page" would

care for my expository method. But as I sized up the situation the important thing was to present the book; one might, if one wished, turn handsprings, juggle apples, or grind a barrel organ, but above all, the reader had a right to determine whether or not he wanted to read the book.

For myself, the last five years with the *World* were wonderful years. Although everything gradually takes on a routine tinge—I am told that even the boatmen in the Vale of Kashmir are exceedingly bored—my adventure never lost its glamour. The *World* was a hive, filled with the activity of healthy men, echoing the clash of ideas. One felt the inspiration of Walter Lippmann's leadership, even if one saw him rarely. Arthur Kroch, who used to be Swope's inveterate companion at the peace conference in Paris, was still there, as assistant to the President; Allan Nevins dashed in and out, capturing a book and leaving a review. F. P. A. went about in shirt sleeves with his brisk, agile step; sometimes he came to talk about World's Fair days in Chicago. I looked with awe upon John O'Hara Cosgrave; after all, he had edited *Everybody's.*

Rollin Kirby, Dudley Nichols, Charles Merz, stopped to chat. I read the columns of Chotzinoff, familiarly known as "Chotzy," but to this day I have never seen him.

I made the usual adjustment in ancestors. In Chicago we used to reminisce about Eugene Field, George Ade, and Finley Peter Dunne. Now I heard at first hand how Hearst took Brisbane; what the *Herald* was like under Bennett; what sort of a reporter Irvin Cobb made on the *Evening*; how Colonel Harvey fired an elevator man who did not carry him direct to his floor; what Walt McDougal put into his cartoons and how Bill Johnston discovered O. Henry, who was always writing another story against the money advanced him. Coming down to these our times, Harry Salpeter told me how Maxwell Anderson had typed his plays between editions among the stacks of the morgue, and how Laurence Stallings had dragged Salpeter from the copy desk to help on books, with the advice that he might lose all his friends if he said what he thought, but by all means to say it.

That is the way the *World* appeared to me. And from our windows on the eleventh floor of

the Pulitzer Building I could see another
world, including the most eager and expectant
readers in America. I had no idea that books
meant life and death to so many people until
I began reviewing them in a slim column seven
days a week. Everywhere, in Manhattan, in
the Bronx and Westchester, in Brooklyn and
on the Jersey side, men took their pens in
hand to make their own comment or to admin-
ister a needed corrective. Sometimes a tired
mind, or carelessness, permitted slips that are
the bane of an editor's life; none ever went by
unnoticed. Sometimes the thought occurred to
readers a continent apart, and one week after
New York had had its say I would hear from
San Diego, or Tucson, or even, months later,
from the Riviera, where forlorn New Yorkers
paid a premium for the *World*. Even though
I knew that many of my readers were sharp-
shooters, I was welcome for their vigilance; I
knew that I was not writing into a void.

These readers helped impress upon me the
unique place of the *World* in American journalism, and although many of us knew that it
was slipping, few of us believed that it would
have to die. I could hardly have felt the trag-

edy as deeply as Mr. White, or Mr. Paulin, or Mr. Heaton, yet I could feel with all of them that we were losing something precious. While we waited, unsettled, for the returns from the court, I was in no mood to write reminiscently. The First Reader of that final day was like unto all the others preceding. And on that last day when the paper carried the message of its sale, I looked for a space out of my windows and beheld the skyline that had grown higher and higher since I came, and the East River almost shut out from sight by the tall towers; then I turned back to my typewriter and put in fresh paper. For The First Reader was going on—and it was right and proper that it should. There was copy due, within twelve hours, for a new edition, on a new day.

EDITORIAL

Concerning Abraham's Bosom

IT OCCURS to us as an afterthought that in all the Jeremiads on the passing of the *World* there may be some unfairness toward the Scripps-Howard interests, in whose bosom the *World* newspapers now lie. Whether they are actually dead, merely sleeping, or very much alive is a question that none of us, late of the *World* staff, can determine. For us it was indeed the end of the *World*, but, after all, that is only our personal feeling.

One of the principles laid down in the *World* office for covering any story was to be fair as well as terse and accurate, and to give both sides in every controversy. The editor of *The End of the World*, recognizing these principles, would be glad to print in full a statement by Roy W. Howard. The Scripps-Howard chairman gave us a statement, but the literary limitations of this book prevent its full publication. The publishers feel that such a statement would be out of harmony with the whole tone and concept of *The End of the World.* Furthermore, it is felt that the Scripps-Howard position was fully published in the newspapers at the time of the sale.

Mr. Howard, however, says several things in his statement to us that are worth preserving. One of them is that some of the newspapers which "are now shedding crocodile tears for the *World* never had a word of commendation for the paper during its entire history under the Pulitzer house flag."

He also says:

So far as we of the Scripps-Howard were concerned and with no disposition to resent or quarrel with those who, for the moment at least, found themselves unable to share our belief that the *World* as an institution was not passing from the journalistic stage, we could understand and were tolerant with (in fact were rather thrilled by) the loyalty to an ideal which was so sincere that it was disposed to regard as profane those hands which we put forward to protect the flickering spark of a journalistic life that was ebbing fast.

The *World* did not end. Its spirit was beckoned to and moved to new quarters.

No man now living made the *World.* No man

can say that its sale to Scripps-Howard marked
the end of the *World*. Only time will reveal whether
a transfer in ownership meant the end or the
rejuvenation.

OBITUARY

By Samuel Kan

Reporter on the World

FEBRUARY 27, 1931.—The *World*, a staunch liberal of enduring journalistic fame died at its home, 63 Park Row, early this morning after a three-day illness, brought on by complications which set in some years ago.

Although the famous newspaper's death had been imminent for three days, almost 3,000 survivors and a host of friends from the Atlantic to the Pacific rallied around the old liberal organ in a last-minute attempt to preserve its life. A few minutes after midnight, however, Surrogate James A. Foley, the chief physician, gave up hope, and ten minutes later the old veteran passed on to the land of merger.

According to Herbert, Joseph, and Ralph Pulitzer, the three sons of the old newspaper, death was inevitable. It had been causing anx-

iety for some years and recently they decided
to call in several eminent physicians for a hurried consultation.

When Doctors Adolph Ochs of the *Times,*
Paul Block and Ogden Reid of the *Herald
Tribune,* failed to materially aid the old veteran, Dr. Roy Wilson Howard, a young chiro-
practor from the Scripps-Howard institution,
was called in a last-minute attempt to prolong
its life. He immediately called in Surrogate
Foley, an erudite specialist, who pronounced
the case incurable.

The *World,* born in 1860, but a block from
its present home, had never left the neighborhood, although many of its old neighbors and
friends decided to move uptown with the
steady upstream surge of business.

The *World* lost its parents in a succession
of mishaps, and finally was adopted by the
late Joseph Pulitzer, a St. Louis publisher of
renown. The adoption officially took place on
May 10, 1883.

It was one of the most active and intelligent
organs in the United States and was personally
concerned with everything that went on in
every corner of the globe. It rose to immense

heights because it exposed corruption, told the truth, wrangled with politicians and political organizations and, in short, feared no one.

To the very last, the *World* was conscious of itself and, despite the pronouncements of Doctors Howard and Foley, managed to keep interested in the doings of one Vivian Gordon, who was murdered the day before its own death; the doings of former-Judge Seabury, the vice investigator; the bubble of the Bank of the United States; and other matters of world importance at that time.

For five hours before it closed its eyes the *World* was surrounded by its 2,867 children, most of whom received two weeks' compensation in the paper's will. Several hundred of the children, who went along to the mausoleum as a guard of honor, did not receive this compensation.

The *World*, besides taking active leadership in national, state, and local affairs, was a member of the Associated Press, the United Press, City News Association, Standard News Association, and the North American Newspaper Alliance. It was the founder of the Yosian Brotherhood and other kindred societies.

Post-mortem services were sung the night of its demise, in Daly's parlors on William Street, with many of its children in attendance. Cardinal Renaud and Bishop Barrett, assisted by the several pastors of the various departments, conducted the solemn ritual. A funeral breakfast was served in Childs!

Services will be held on the date of publication of this book. Meanwhile the body rests at 73 Dey Street at the parlors of Scripps-Howard Alliance.

The family requests that flowers be omitted.

FINIS MUNDI